STEAMING INTO THE FIRING LINE

Tales of the Footplate in Wartime Britain

Michael Clutterbuck

HEDDON PUBLISHING

www.heddonpublishing.com
www.facebook.com/heddonpublishing
@PublishHeddon

This series is dedicated to my late father, William Harold Clutterbuck, himself a railwayman. In giving his son a Hornby train in 1937, he passed on a bug which still claims me firmly. My only regret is that he is no longer with us to see the results. Thank you, Dad, for all you did for us.

Introduction

I originally wrote these short stories for my own entertainment. The characters are, of course, completely fictitious and bear no relation to anyone I knew. However, the locomotive sheds existed, as did other features of the railways in the 1940s. The coalnet in the back yard in Chapter Eleven is also noted by Harold Gasson in the autobiographical account of his days as a fireman (and firing days, footplate days and nostalgic days), which is well worth reading.

As the son of a Chester railwayman, I still clearly remember my train-spotting days in the late forties and early fifties of the twentieth century. Some of the minor details in the stories also have a basis of truth in them. For example, Dad privately admitted responsibility for dealing with the difficult passenger outside Prestatyn in Chapter Ten; and I was one of the "little buggers" whose behaviour encouraged Lance to develop his new skill in Chapter Eleven.

My main aim in writing has been to recall a few of the difficulties and dangers in the lives of enginemen during wartime. The need for the Blackout during the war made their jobs more difficult. The men had to pull a tarpaulin over their cabs at night to hide the glow of the fire from enemy aircraft overhead. This often made the cabs very hot and unpleasant places to work in. Furthermore, not only were the railway centres heavily bombed, but trains themselves, both freight and passenger, were a prime target and were often bombed or machine-gunned.

The work was physically very demanding, especially for the fireman. Even as late as the 1960s, any fireman on the crack West of England expresses would need to shovel a ton of coal per hour for every one of the four hours needed to reach Plymouth. Furthermore, to be effective it would have to be placed exactly where it was needed. This was frequently twelve feet down the firebox in a King class locomotive.

A driver with a heavy hand on the regulator (and there

were plenty) could pull great holes in a fireman's carefully built-up fire, which would then have to be repaired if steam pressure was to be maintained. The fireman would then be required to do the same thing the following day on his return to Paddington. This was assuming the engine was in good condition; if it wasn't, then more heavy shovelling would be necessary. The fireman's job was very hard, as not only did he have to keep the firebox fed but he also had to ensure that the boiler was properly topped up and the steam pressure maintained in order for the driver to do his job. The fireman also had to keep an eye on the signals and warn the driver about their status.

These days, reminiscences often glamorize the profession, yet when the diesels arrived in the 1950s and '60s, enginemen were generally only too thankful to put away their shovels and oilcans, knowing that their collar and tie would remain clean for the whole of their shifts. There is no doubt that steam locomotives still evince a romance which is scarcely matched by any other obsolete mode of transport, with the possible exception of sailing ships (although whether sail is obsolete is a moot point) but the 'romance of steam' is almost entirely in the minds of those who didn't have to spend their lives in a dirty, draughty, rattling cab.
   I am nevertheless grateful for having been privileged to live at least the first part of my life in a time when most trains were hauled by steam locomotives, yet in hindsight, equally thankful that I took my father's advice in 1960 not to join the railways; modelling them is good enough for me.

Mike Clutterbuck
Melbourne,
Australia.

Steaming into the Firing Line
Tales of the Footplate in Wartime Britain

1 - There's trouble brewing (September 1939)

"Half the poor little sods don't know what's going on," commented the fireman of the Hall class 4-6-0 at the head of the train. From his position in the cab, he was looking back along the platform at Birkenhead Woodside.

The station was heaving with children, all wearing their names on labels hung around their necks and carrying little square cardboard boxes containing their gasmasks. The children's ages varied, from about four years old up to twelve or thirteen. Accompanying them were a wide variety of small cases. Harassed officials tried to chivvy their charges into groups, the better to keep an eye on them, whilst the railway staff looked on in wonderment.

The children were being evacuated from Merseyside, and the long train was to take them to parts of the country which the government hoped would not get the attention of the Luftwaffe. The train was due to call at Wrexham, Ruabon and Llangollen, before dividing at Corwen with coaches for Barmouth, Pwllheli and Aberystwyth. The Hall and its enginemen, Driver George Denton and Passed Cleaner Lance Hargreaves, would take the train as far as Corwen, shedding children and coaches along the route.

The two enginemen in the cab of the Hall were very different characters, yet for some time now they had been working together smoothly. George Denton was in his middle fifties, was short in stature, and looked as if he would be at home in an office. His heavy driver's jacket and trousers were clean; quite an achievement in the cab of a steam locomotive. George was an experienced and very competent engineman; neat in appearance and with an easy-going manner. He was also firm and controlled whenever a situation developed in the cab – an occurrence not as uncommon as one might think. A 70-ton steam locomotive could be as temperamental as any stage or film actor, and needed careful handling at all times by both crewmen. George knew most of the idiosyncrasies that Great Western Railway locomotives were capable of and also knew what to do when they showed up.

The Hall's fireman, Lance Hargreaves, was also short but his arms were well-muscled. He was very young, barely seventeen, yet was already a Passed Cleaner, meaning he was permitted to work as a fireman under training. In George's opinion, Lance would easily pass his fireman's examination. In spite of his rough manners and (it must be admitted) his earthy vocabulary, he was already showing an unusual flair for work in the cab of a steam locomotive. Lance's natural exuberance was a bonus in the eyes of his driver, who was kindly and tolerant.

Lance was stocky and his broad shoulders gave him the strength to manipulate the fireman's main tool, the shovel, with ease. In between his shovelling, he was also learning other crucial skills: keeping an eye on the various gauges; glancing occasionally down the train for hot boxes or other problems such as parted couplings; getting into the tender to break up the large lumps of coal which wouldn't otherwise fit into the fire hole; breaking up any clinker in the firebox.

Lance was rapidly discovering that keeping enough steam pressure in the boiler for the driver to do his work wasn't anything like as easy as just shovelling coal in. A fireman's work was far more complex and taxing than that.

The Hall was a Special and considerably longer than the usual passenger trains starting from Woodside. Normally even the Paddington expresses would consist of only six or seven coaches hauled by a large Prairie class tank engine. This would take the train to Chester, where it would enter Number Two bay platform. There it would be strengthened by another three or four coaches with a big Castle or Star 4-6-0 express locomotive, and move southwards in the reverse direction. The train would then travel to Wolverhampton Low Level, where the locomotive would be changed again and the train would be strengthened once more with another half dozen coaches before being taken on to Paddington.

This train, however, being an evacuation special, was heading for Central Wales.

There was a tapping sound coming nearer as a wheel tapper made his way along the track, stopping to bend down and tap each wheel, listening to the sound.

"I've often wondered, Mr D.," queried Lance, "Wot the 'ell's 'e doin' that for?"

The wheel tapper had finished and, with his long-handled hammer slung over his shoulder, was walking past them to another train.

"He's checking for metal fatigue, Lance," answered the driver, "We don't want any wheels breaking while we're running."

"Well why doesn't 'e 'ave a good butcher's then? 'E'd soon see if a wheel's cracked."

"No, he probably wouldn't. The cracks are very fine indeed, so listening is the best way."

"Well, I reckon it's daft. If yer go round beltin' the wheels with a 'ammer, yer goin' ter break a few! Stands ter reason." Lance looked at George triumphantly.

"Ever heard the expression 'sound as a bell', Lance?"

Lance frowned; "Course I 'ave. It means everythin's 'unky dory."

"Why?"

"Why wot?"

"Why is it hunky-dory? Think about it – how does your Ma tell if one of her plates is cracked?"

"Er- she taps it... Oh, yeah, it's the same idea, innit? Mind you, I'd still be 'appier if 'e didn't 'it 'em so 'ard."

George chuckled. "I hope Sid Thomson lets me keep you as my mate, Lance, you're a breath of fresh air!"

Lance smiled as he bent to check the fire. He enjoyed working with George Denton, and was happy that his driver was pleased, even if he had no idea why.

When the last wailing child had been separated from its mother and urged into a coach, the guard waved his green flag and Lance, watching for it, turned to his driver.

"We've got the green, Mr D."

George nodded, released the brake, and began to ease up the long regulator lever. The big engine slowly moved off along the left hand curve out of Woodside. Picking up speed, they were soon passing the joint LMS and GWR engine sheds on their left. They passed Rockferry station where the Mersey Railway electrics terminated for their passengers to change platforms. But the special did not stop. It steamed smoothly past the crowds waiting to board the regular trains to Chester and all points south.

They passed the busy shipbuilding and industrial towns of Bromborough and Port Sunlight and sped past Hooton where the Ellesmere Port and Neston branches left the main line on either side. Soon they entered the pretty, rural parts of the Wirral past Capenhurst, Mollington and Upton-by-Chester, before bypassing Chester General station on the cut-off curve, carrying on to the main LMS line to North Wales. They ran through the two tunnels and under the corner of the City Walls before crossing the Dee bridge; the scene of a serious accident a hundred years earlier when the bridge had collapsed, dropping most of a train with its passengers into the river.

In the Curzon Park cutting, a red LMS 4-4-0 Compound with a holiday express of eight corridors hurried past in the opposite direction on its way to Birmingham.

"There won't be too many more of those holiday trains for a while," commented George as it passed.

At Saltney Junction, the train rejoined GWR metals to the south and they began to pick up speed past Balderton, in order to be able to get a good run up Gresford Bank. Lance was by now shovelling hard to keep the steam up, and when they pulled in at Wrexham, he breathed a sigh of relief.

"We're dropping a couple of coaches here, Lance, so we've time for a quick brew up. You look like you need

4

one," said George.

"Ta, Mr D., I won't say no to a cuppa," replied Lance.

He reached for the tea can, took the lid off, poured a couple of teaspoons full of tea leaves in and grabbed his shovel, pushing it into the fire, flattening the bed near the fire hole. He then carefully slid the can onto the flat area with the coal pick handle and shut the fire door.

George picked up a milk bottle from the toolbox and a bag of sugar and held them ready as Lance opened the fire door again and fished out the can. The water was already boiling. Lance then wrapped a piece of cotton waste round the can handle and George poured some milk into the can, then Lance swung the can round a few times to stir the tea.

"Righto, Mr D., let's 'ave yer mug." Lance filled his driver's mug and then his own, adding sugar to his. George did not take sugar; a legacy of living through the First World War.

On the platform, accompanying adults were trying to comfort children before handing them over to other waiting supervisors who were checking labels and guiding the confused children towards buses and the few waiting mothers who had agreed to look after the evacuees. While they were waiting, a loud clanking sound could be heard. Lance looked out of the cab to see an old Aberdare class 2-6-0 goods engine with a train of khaki trucks and tanks heading north.

"An Army train for Liverpool," said George as the Aberdare passed their cab, "There'll be plenty more trains like that soon, and my lad, we'll likely be crewing some of them."

"But not with an old kettle like that, I 'ope," said Lance, gazing at the locomotive.

"Yes, those Aberdares are almost forty years old and should be scrapped, but now that we have a war on, they'll carry on a bit longer, I bet. They're not as fancy as this Hall we've got, but they are strong; I've driven a few of them and they're not as bad as they look."

The guard's whistle blew and George eased the regulator open. The engine moved off smoothly, but as it passed the Croes Newydd shed, there was a loud *crack!* The water gauge glass blew out. George watched in surprise as Lance immediately dropped his shovel, turned, and smartly fitted a new glass from his bag.

"Well done, Lance," said George, "You're learning; but what if it went again?"

"No problem, Mr D.," replied Lance, "I've got another spare in me bag."

George nodded. Satisfied. Passed Cleaner Hargreaves had the makings of a first class fireman.

At Ruabon they turned off the GWR main line on to the Dee valley route and paused at Llangollen for more children to get off. George nodded at the crowds of children on the platform, "There'll be some language problems here – those kids with their Merseyside accents will have difficulties with the locals here, even if they speak English – which a few of them don't."

"The kids'll manage," said Lance, "An' if they stay long enough, they'll 'ave two languages."

George was surprised again, "Very perceptive of you," he commented.

Lance bent happily to his shovelling; he hadn't realized he was 'perceptive'. He didn't know what it meant but it sounded good.

At Corwen, the train was divided as planned. Lance and George left their engine to a new crew.

The new driver rubbed his hands in anticipation, "A Hall, eh? We don't often get our hands on one of these down here. Is it permitted?"

"That's a point," said George scratching his head, "You'd better get a move on quickly before Authority notices. It's a D red engine and this is a blue route."

GWR engines were classified according to their weight into red, blue, yellow and uncoloured routes. Each had small discs of the appropriate colour painted on their cab sides. With its new crew, the train got as far as Dolgellau before an inspector noticed and the engine was taken off and replaced by a lighter 43 class 2-6-0.

Back at Corwen, George and Lance were scheduled to return to Chester with a short freight. When he saw the engine arriving from Barmouth, George smiled. It was another elderly Aberdare class 2-6-0 and it was pulling a train of army lorries and tanks. The coupling rods clanked around the outside frames, giving the locomotive a very old fashioned, almost tank-like appearance. George could see from the smoke that the engine appeared to be steaming satisfactorily.

"Now, Lance," he grinned at his fireman as the engine stopped to change crews, "Let's see if you can boil this old kettle!"

The run back to Chester showed Lance that the 'old kettle' was still quite capable of doing its work without any fuss. They took it to the shed, leaving their freight for an LMS 4F 0-6-0 to back on and take the tanks on to Liverpool docks.

In Chester, George spoke to Sid Thomson the shedmaster about taking the Hall to Corwen.

"Mmm... yes, that's right; I forgot that Halls are D reds," said Sid thoughtfully, "That Hall is one of ours too, we were responsible. Look, don't worry about it George. Now there's a war on, all kinds of slips are going to be made. If anyone asks, tell them to see me; that'll give me time to think of something!"

"Wotcher tell the boss for?" asked Lance later as they clocked off their shift, "'E could've fined yer or somethin'." He pulled out a chocolate bar and began to nibble at it.

"No, he wouldn't, Sid's not like that. Like me, Sid was in the Great War and one thing we both learned was that if you knew trouble was on its way you could be ready for it – saved our hides many a time. And it's just as true on the Great Western Railway!"

"I'll remember that!" commented Lance.

"And enjoy your chocolate bar while you can," said George, "If this war follows the pattern of the last lot, you won't see too many of those in the future."

"Nah," said Lance dismissively, "The Jerries are busy in Poland, and then the Frogs 'ave got an army waitin' for 'em just as big as their own, *an'* there's the British Expeditionary Force as well. Me Dad says our blokes in the BEF'll be back 'ome before Christmas."

George shook his head, "They said that in '14 and look what happened. Believe me, I know the Germans; they're sure to have something up their sleeves. In early 1918, when everyone said they were on the brink of losing, they gave us a hell of a fright. No lad, we're all going to have to learn to tighten our belts and do without luxuries for a lengthy spell, if you ask me."

2 - Get your facts right! (June 1940)

The driver of the long troop train eased his Grange class 4-6-0 round the left hand curve at the Hawthorns Halt just before West Bromwich, where the line to Kidderminster and Bewdley left the main Birkenhead line. As they gradually left the Black Country, with its smoky air and barrage balloons in the sky like huge, silver-grey beetles, the scenery began to change into a more rural setting. Their first stop was at Kidderminster.

"Look at the poor buggers!"

Driver Gorton leaned out of his cab, eyeing the bedraggled troops as they detrained onto the platform. Many of them were bandaged, some were using crutches, and all had an air of gloom which matched the relentless drizzle which had not ceased all day. In the car park outside the station there were several buses and charabancs waiting to take some of the troops further on, to other army depots or local hospitals.

A platform inspector climbed into the cab, "You'll likely be here for at least half an hour, driver, so you might as well make a brew for yourself and your mate."

"Yeah, right, thanks for the warning." Harry Gorton was in his early sixties, but he was clearly still fit enough to handle the duties of an engine driver.

"You hear that, Ferdy?" he asked his fireman, "Get the tea can into the fire, and we'll have a brew up while we're standing here."

"Righto!" replied Ferdinand Harrison. He put the can onto his shovel and carefully placed them into the firebox before collecting the tea and milk from the tender toolbox.

"I'm just popping off for a quick bog," said Harry, climbing down from the cab, "I'll be back in two shakes of a lamb's tail."

9

Harry saw an RAF Wing Commander walking towards him. As he was about to enter the toilet he heard one of the sergeants mutter to his men, "Bloody RAF, where were those buggers when we was gettin' shot at on the beach at Dunkirk?"

The officer stopped sharply, turned and looked at the sergeant.

"What was that?"

The sergeant looked up, "Er, nothin'."

"Nothing, *Sir*!"

"Nothin', Sir!"

Harry reached the toilet and went inside. He heard the officer snap, "Come with me, Sergeant! Away from your men."

Judging from their steps, the two came to a stop just outside the toilet, where Harry could clearly hear all they said.

"Tell me, Sergeant, why are you not in France, still?"

"The Army got us out, sir."

"No it didn't, the Army was defeated. The *Navy* got you out. How many men did your unit lose in France?"

"About twenty per cent, Sir."

"So, most of you got away? Now let me give a few facts. The RAF was patrolling the skies above the beach trying to keep the bombers off you people. Last week there were 24 pilots and 16 Hurricanes in one of my squadrons; today there are two planes and five pilots left; the others are dead, POWs or in German hospitals."

"I'm sorry about that, sir," Harry thought the sergeant sounded genuinely regretful.

"Wait; there's more. The Hurricane is a good plane, but it's no match for an ME 109; my pilots were brave men but many only had 20 hours in Hurries. The German pilots are damn good and very well trained, they are battle hardened from Spain and Poland, and there are five of them to every one of ours; so we were defeated too. Now, if you want to be a leader of men, get your facts straight. And as far as bravery is concerned, you and I in the Armed Forces are trained to be brave. Last week I saw an old sailor in a tiny launch, the *Saucy Sue*, trips round the bay for one and six. He took his cockleshell across the Channel five times before it was machine gunned."

"What happened to him?"

"He got picked up by an RAF Sea Rescue launch. Now before you make any more cracks about people get your facts straight!"

"No Sir; yes Sir!"

"Oh, and Sergeant?"

"Sir?"

"Just forget those details I told you."

"While I was sitting on the bog, I heard an RAF officer give an army sergeant a right old bollocking!" Harry had returned to his cab and was drinking his tea.

"Why, what had the sergeant done?" asked Ferdy in surprise.

"He thought the RAF had done nothing to help the boys at Dunkirk."

"Well that's what I heard too."

"We might have heard wrong."

The platform inspector came up to the cab again, "We're finished here, Driver, so as soon as the line's clear, you can move off again to Salop."

They waited as a big 47xx 2-8-0 with a long, unfitted goods hurried through the station; it cleared the section and their own starter signal dropped to the 'clear' position.

"We've got the clear, Harry," said the fireman and Harry lifted the regulator, easing the heavy train away from the platform. They were on their way to Shrewsbury, known in railway terms as 'Salop'.

"Things are changing round here, Ferdy," he commented, as their train crossed the points at the end of the station to enter the single tracked section. "Kidderminster doesn't see Granges and 47s too often. Heavy fitted freights and long passenger trains make a change from the usual diesel railcars or short mixed goods with a Pannier or a 22 in front. Now that we've been at war for nearly a year the main line between Birmingham and Salop is so busy, they have to use this as an alternate route. This sleepy little route may have to get used to being a busy line!"

While Harry was explaining this to his fireman, he was leaning on the ledge of the cab side and looking out. This was extremely fortunate because as the goods passed, Harry realized that the guard's van was missing. Quick as a thought, he dropped the regulator, slammed on the brake as well as the tender brakes and tugged the whistle chain urgently. His train came to a sudden standstill and in the distance he saw three wagons and a brake van rolling slowly towards them on the same track.

As the locomotive slowed unexpectedly, Ferdy almost lost his balance and tipped the load of coal he was carrying all over the cab floor. He stared at his driver.

"What the hell?" he called, startled, then glanced out of the left cab front window, "Gawdalmighty!"

The train had stopped with a jerk and a few moments later the runaway vehicles hit the front buffers of their engine with a loud *Clang!*

There didn't seem to be any obvious damage to either their locomotive or the wagons, but Harry said, "Quick, Ferdy, go and check on the goods guard, he may have been hurt."

Ferdy climbed hurriedly down and ran along the loose wagons towards the steps of the guard's van, but before he reached it, he turned with a grin on his face and walked back to the cab, calling "Harry, the guard's not happy, but he's not hurt!"

"How do you know?"

"You should hear the language coming from inside the van! He obviously wasn't aware that his train had parted."

Hearing Harry's frantic whistle, the driver of the freight engine had stopped and had now realized that his train had parted. He was berating his own fireman fiercely, perhaps trying to gloss over the fact that it was the job of both crewmen to check that their train stayed complete. It took almost an hour for the matter to finally get sorted, and both crews sighed over the thought of all the reports and other paperwork in front of them at the end of their shifts. The runaway wagons and guard's van were shunted into a siding to be checked for damage, and a spare brakevan was quickly found for the guard of the freight before they could all get away again.

The scene later on the platform at Bewdley was almost a repeat of that at Kidderminster. Depressed soldiers filled the platform and were ferried onto buses.

This time, however, the wait for Harry and Ferdy was not very long and the train moved off to its final destination. Arriving in Shrewsbury, Ferdy climbed down from the cab to uncouple the Grange from the troop train, while a big Prairie buffered up at the tail end to draw the coaches back into the carriage sidings extending along the main line to Hereford and Cardiff.

Harry and Ferdy handed their engine over to a waiting Salop crew after assuring them that the engine, in spite of the minor fracas in Kidderminster, was in good nick and could handle whatever Control wanted to tie on it. They began the long walk along the tracks to the GWR shed at Coleham; on their way to the enginemen's mess shed they passed a grimy Hall class 4-6-0.

"Look at that, Harry!" said Ferdy in disgust, "That's one of ours and it's filthy! I bet it hasn't been cleaned for a month."

"No," they heard a voice behind them and turned to see the Salop shedmaster, "And it's not going to be cleaned now either. You lads are taking it back to Snow Hill with some Empty Coaching Stock."

Harry took out his watch from his waistcoat pocket and glanced at it. "Thanks, another 45 minutes should finish off our shift nicely," he said to the foreman, then paused, frowning; "Hang on, we just passed the carriage sidings and I didn't see any ECS there."

"No," said the shedmaster, "You'd need good eyesight to see them, they're in Chester. You'll have to go Light Engine and pick them up from there. And," he paused, seeing their faces, "Before you ask, these instructions come from your foreman at Tyseley; he's just been on the line to me."

The light engine run to Chester took just under an hour and as they pulled into the Chester reversing triangle, Ferdy and Harry saw a long rake of green Southern Railway stock in the sidings alongside the Birkenhead avoiding tracks.

"But we'll be well over our shift!" complained Harry to Sid Thomson, the Chester shed foreman, as they reported to him.

"We're all having to work a bit harder these days," the latter responded unsympathetically, "Don't you know there's a war on? Those coaches are urgently needed in Plymouth Millbay."

Ferdy and Harry took their engine to the turntable, grumbling at the foreman's comments.

"Who does he think he is?" said Harry, but as he spoke, he was overheard by a passing engineman.

"Harry Gorton!" said the other man, "Haven't seen you for a while."

"Oh, er, hello Ted," Harry turned to his fireman, "This is Ted Simmons, Ferdy. He's a Chester driver." Harry told Ted why they were unhappy at having to do an extended shift.

"Aye, well don't knock Sid Thomson," advised Ted, "Sid's a good bloke, but ever since this Dunkirk shemozzle started a fortnight back, he's been doing 18 and 20 hours a day. He's got a little straw palliasse in his office which he kips on, and he hasn't seen his missus or had a decent meal for a week. He's knackered, like the rest of us, but carries on."

"Hmm," replied Harry, "Well we didn't know that."

14

"No, of course not Harry, but before you make any more cracks about people, get your facts straight!" Ted marched off.

Harry looking after the disappearing Ted, turned to his fireman and said, "Second time I've heard that today, Ferdy."

"I read that the Jerries'll be bombing us soon," commented Ferdy.

"Bombing?" Harry snorted derisively. "You shouldn't believe all you read in that rag of a paper you're fond of!"

"Well what about all them barrage balloons we see everywhere these days?"

"That's just the government pretending to be organized. They're a waste of time; there won't be any bombing. The Jerries know perfectly well that if they bomb us, we'll bomb them back."

Two very weary enginemen brought their empty coaching stock train into Snow Hill where a Castle class 4-6-0 was waiting to take it on to Plymouth. The replacement crew from Laira shed in Plymouth showed little sympathy when they heard about the long shift; they too had been on duty for ten hours already and were expecting to need at least five more to Millbay.

As they were taking the Hall back to Tyseley shed, Harry glanced out of the cab and called to Ferdy, "Hey, look at that!"

"What?" asked Ferdy, coming over to Harry's side of the cab. In a neighbouring suburban street there were three houses in smoking ruins with two ambulances ferrying the injured away.

"What in hell's happened there?" Harry couldn't believe his eyes at the destruction.

"That's bomb damage!" gasped Ferdy.

"Don't be silly, Ferdy, the Germans wouldn't be this far over..." Harry stopped talking as he looked up to the sky.

He could see three large aircraft high up and disappearing into the distance with another smaller aircraft buzzing round them; there was a faint *rat-at-tat!* sound.

He nodded slowly.

"I think you're right for once, Ferdy," he muttered grimly, "It's going to be a long bloody war!"

3 - An emergency shift (September 1940)

As if to defy its reputation for rain, the weather in Manchester on this late September afternoon was glorious. Despite this, the sun was unable to completely disperse the smoke and haze over the city; the consequence of the heavy air raid two days previously.

"Gawd, I'll be glad to get out o' this town!" commented Fireman Jack Metcalfe to his driver as he looked out at the newly bombed-out building on the other side of the road that ran alongside Central Station. They were waiting on the headshunt for permission to back onto their train. Driver Len Rintoule didn't reply; he was watching the big LMS Patriot class 4-6-0 at the head of a St Pancras express on the next platform. The driver saw him from the cab and waved.

"Nice looking engine!" called Len over to the driver.

"Yeah, these 'Baby Scots' are fine engines."

"I heard they were rebuilds of the old LNWR Claughtons," said Len.

"That's what the company accountants tell us," laughed the LMS driver, "But that's cobblers! They were brand new engines; one or two of the first ones had the wheel bosses from withdrawn Claughtons, but that's all."

"Why d'you call them 'Baby Scots'?"

"They look like Scots but they're a bit smaller, but don't let that fool you. When they're in good nick they can give the Scots a run for their money any day."

"Really?"

"Yeah, only last week we deputised for a failed big Pacific at Crewe and took the heavy Anglo-Scottish express on to Euston. We were ten minutes late leaving Crewe after the engine change and got into Euston only twenty minutes late."

"Quite an achievement!" Len was impressed.

The LMS driver asked, "Where are you off to?"

"Chester."

"Chester?" The driver sounded surprised. He studied the side of Len's engine, "I didn't know the LNER was in Chester."

"Oh yes, mind you, we're not really LNER, we're CLC but we use LNER stock."

"CLC?"

"Cheshire Lines Committee."

"I've never seen LNER engines in Chester."

"Ever taken a North Wales train?"

"Of course, many times."

"Then you've been right underneath us; we have a separate station - Chester Northgate, directly over the first tunnel."

Just then, the St Pancras express received the 'all clear' and the driver waved once more then took his train gently away around the right hand curve out of the station.

Len eased his D11 4-4-0 passenger engine back from the headshunt onto the six teak non-corridors of the stopping train in Platform Fourteen. He and his fireman still had about five minutes before they were due out.

"Just look at that!" said Jack to his driver. They both peered over the side of the fence down to the street below; a tram was trundling along past the burnt-out building; the tram had three of the upper deck windows boarded over, the Bovril sign on the side had a long scorch mark along it, and under his cap the driver had a large head bandage.

"You've got to admit, they've got guts just to live here!"

"True enough, but what choice do they have?" replied Len as the platform starter signal clanged up. "OK, Jack, now have we got steam up ready for the off?"

Jack checked the gauges and had a quick glance into the firebox. "Yep, we're right to go, soon's we get the flag."

Just as he spoke, they heard the whistle. Jack peered back down the train. "Righto Len, we've got the green."

Len gradually lifted the regulator and the train moved slowly out of the platform, following the LMS express around the right hand curve and along the viaduct above the streets. They followed the CLC tracks, which were at a slightly lower level from the main lines to the south, before veering off to the left and on through the south-western suburbs of Manchester. They joined the tracks of the electric service to Altrincham.

As they passed Old Trafford, Len commented with a chuckle, "I'm not really a football man, but I once saw United play City here a few years back. The huge crowd wanted blood but all they got was a draw!"

As they passed into the leafier and wealthier suburbs where the evidence of bombing was almost non-existent, Jack said, "If I was a Mancunian, I think I'd like to live here; nice house and garden and you can be in the city centre in twenty minutes."

"On our pay, we'd have to work until we were about 150 before we could earn enough to live here," replied Len, "Still, you're right – it's a very nice area. Mind you, Delamere'd be my choice. I like bird watching and Delamere Forest has plenty of variety."

"Checking out birds? I'm surprised at you, Len, a man of your age – and happily married too. What would your missus think?"

Len grinned as they pulled in to stop at Altrincham, the terminus of the electric service. Once clear of Altrincham signal box and the slow curve, the D11 rapidly picked up speed. It sprinted through the picturesque station and glorious village of Hale, before plunging into rich farming countryside and sweeping past the fabled village of Knutsford.

Later, as they entered the salt mining industrial complex, Len called out, "Lostock distant at danger, Jack."

The pair had worked together for several years and their established teamwork swung smoothly into action. Jack put down his shovel and immediately began to fill the coal bucket with carefully chosen small lumps of coal. Len handed him the empty tea can which Jack placed near the bucket. As they pulled up in Lostock Gralam, Jack took the bucket and can, climbed down to the platform and crossed to the signal box, where he went up the steps, opened the door and entered.

"Morning, Jim," he said to the signalman, handing him the empty tea can and putting the bucket of coal near the heating stove.

"Morning, Jack. Ta for the coal. I won't need it yet, but my mate on night shift'll be glad of it." He filled the tea can with fresh hot water from his tap and gave it to Jack.

"Thanks," said the fireman, "This'll taste better than our water from the tender." He returned to the cab, placing the tea can on the firehole shelf.

"We'll brew up at Northwich," said Len as they pulled away from the station.

Shortly after, as they reached the Cheshire town, the largest between Altrincham and Chester, Len placed the tea can carefully into the small hollow that Jack had already made in the fire. The water boiled in seconds and the can was pulled out, the tea thrown in and swirled around. The two mugs were ready with milk; Len much preferred his tea sweet, but sugar rationing precluded such luxuries. The mugs of tea were made and drunk while the porters transferred parcels and various other items of luggage from and to the luggage van.

The platform was full with a sprinkling of military uniforms, businessmen from Manchester, and women returning with their weekly shopping.

"You know, if I was in a hurry to go to Manchester from Chester," commented Jack, "I'd go from Chester General with the LMS; they've got the fast club trains from Llandudno which take under an hour to Exchange. Nothing on this line takes less than about ninety minutes!"

"Yes, that's true, but think of the advantages of our route."

"What advantages?"

"Well when we stop at little country villages like

Mouldsworth, Cuddington and Delamere you can almost forget the war for a while."

When they pulled in at Delamere, they saw a party of a dozen schoolchildren sitting waiting for the train. The teacher was admonishing a little boy.

"Jeffrey Hawkins, you pick up that sandwich wrapping paper this instant! It's only been used once; take it home and your mother can use it again tomorrow. And if I catch you littering again, I'll be round to your house to speak to your father!"

Young Hawkins picked up the wrapping paper and put it into his cardboard gas mask box which, like all the other children, he had tied with string and slung over his shoulder. He made a face at the back of the retreating teacher.

"And don't make rude faces behind my back!" she continued without turning round.

Jack, hearing this, laughed and commented to Len, "D'you know, I remember my teacher once saying exactly the same thing to me half way through the Great War. We lived in Wigan at the time, and that day the schoolteacher had taken us all blackberrying."

He looked once more at the little station building, the few people on the platform, the teacher chivvying the children on to the train and the forest surrounding the station area. "Still, you're right about one thing; it's easy to forget the war in a place like this."

However, a few minutes later, as they were passing the Mickle Trafford junction with the GWR/LMS joint line to Warrington, they watched as a Great Western 2-8-0 freight engine passed them travelling north with a long train of flat wagons loaded with tanks, lorries and heavy anti-aircraft guns.

Len sighed. "I knew the peaceful scene couldn't last!"

They finally pulled into Chester Northgate and watched as the teacher marched her brood down the platform, but she stopped suddenly when one of the children said something to her.

"Oh, my goodness, you're quite right, Jennifer, I completely forgot! Right children, stop here for a moment."

The line of children stopped, and the teacher said, "Quickly now! Gas mask practice!"

The children removed the gas masks from the boxes they carried everywhere, putting them on while the teacher went round and checked that each was being applied properly.

"Very good, children, now you can take them off again and put them back in your boxes."

With that, she marched them all off again, past the front of the locomotive, and out at the station exit.

The following morning, Len was woken by a knocking at the front door of his house in Brook Lane.

"What the hell?" he swore as he saw on the alarm clock that it was ten minutes to four. Struggling into his dressing gown, he stumbled downstairs, opened the front door and was about to give the visitor a vigorous piece of his mind, when he saw that it was young Tarbuck, the Northgate shed's knocker up lad.

"Very sorry, Mr Rintoule, but you're wanted now at Northgate. Mr Metcalfe is wanted as well; I'm just going to get him."

"What's up, lad?"

"Not sure, but I think there's an emergency; they're getting an engine ready for you."

"I'll be right there," Len said to the lad, before calling upstairs to his wife, "Betty, there's some problem at Northgate. Jack and I are needed there now."

"Your sandwiches are ready packed on the kitchen table, Len; don't forget to take them."

"Ta, Love. I'm not sure what time I'll be home again."

Len hurried to get dressed and was walking up the road in ten minutes.

On arrival at Northgate, the shed night foreman said,

"Mornin', Len; I'm sorry to get you out at this ungodly hour but there's been an emergency. Manchester copped a heavy raid again last night and there's a train with injured heading our way. You're to go and pick it up in Northwich at 5.35 and bring it here. A Manchester crew have volunteered to stay on their shift and bring the train as far as Northwich, but they're both knackered and will have to get back home – that's if the poor buggers have got a home to go to."

"So what have you got for us?"

"There's a D11 coaled up and ready. You'll take it light engine to Northwich and bring the train back here; they tell me it has nine coaches."

"Doesn't sound too much of a problem for a D11."

"Yeah, well, that's only the start. We detach four of the coaches here and the injured will be taken to the Royal Infirmary for treatment. We're trying to organize other arrangements for the remaining five coaches. The Infirmary can't handle them all."

At 5.25, Len and Jack pulled in at Northwich shed, turned their engine, and backed on to the heavy train full of injured. One coach had already been detached as its injured were being transferred to waiting ambulances. Several stretchers were laid out on the platform with the bodies covered in blankets. Nurses and doctors were going through the coaches, checking on their patients, many of whom had to be laid out on the floors of the compartments. One of the doctors came over to Len and asked, "How long before we can get these patients into hospital?"

"I'm told we'll have a clear road to Chester," replied Len, "So we'll make the best possible speed with no stops – should be there in less than half an hour. But the hospital in Chester can only take the first four coach loads; the rest will be moved on elsewhere."

"We'd better get the most badly hurt into the first four coaches then, can you hang on till we're organized?"

"Sure, we'll wait till you give us the all clear."

Len and Jack watched as several stretcher cases were exchanged, and after ten minutes the doctor came up again.

"We've got the most urgent cases in the first four coaches, so we're ready when you are."

Jack leaned out for the guard's wave and whistle, and Len lifted the regulator as soon as Jack gave him the signal.

As they pulled into the Northgate terminus, they noticed a C 13 4-4-2 tank engine waiting on the release track. As soon as they stopped at the buffers, the shed foreman climbed into their cab. More orderlies and nurses hurried along the platform to help with the injured, and several ambulances were waiting in the station forecourt.

Len noticed three covered stretchers placed gently at the side of the platform; patients who no longer needed medical aid.

"Sorry, lads," the foreman said, "More work for you. Leave the D11 here, I've got a spare crew to take it and service it. I want you two to take the C13 with the remaining coaches to Wrexham. You'll have a clear run again, non-stop to Wrexham Exchange where three coaches will be detached and handed over to the Great Western. They'll have a loco waiting there; you'll be left with the last two to take on to Wrexham Central."

At Wrexham Exchange, they again saw several hospital staff waiting for them as a Great Western pannier tank backed on to the rear of their train. The last three coaches were drawn off and the pannier soon had them crossing to the Great Western side of the station. As soon as the coaches were detached, Len lifted the regulator and pulled away out of Exchange, down the curve under the Great Western main line and into Wrexham Central, where more hospital staff and ambulances were waiting. The Wrexham stationmaster came over and thanked them after the last of the injured had been taken away.

"Where have the Great Western taken the other three

coaches?" asked Jack.

"They'll detach one at Ruabon and the other two will go on to Oswestry. Now you two can go and grab yourselves a cup of tea in the staff canteen. You've got a bit of a wait; you are to pick up the three coaches again as soon as the GWR can bring them back to Exchange and take them with the two here back to Chester for cleaning up. They'll have blood and used bandages all over the floor. I'll give you both a call twenty minutes before the GWR arrive in Exchange."

Both Len and Jack were silent in the staff canteen, subdued by what they had seen in the last couple of hours. The doctors, nurses and orderlies had all been professional and efficient in looking after the injured, but both men had noticed at least a dozen stretcher cases of patients who had been beyond help. The stationmaster came into the canteen and sat down at their table, bringing his own mug of tea.

"Many thanks again for today, lads," he said, sliding a thin bottle from out of his pocket. He poured a short measure into both of their mugs and then one into his own. "You've seen things today that railwaymen don't normally have to put up with. Unfortunately, you may see the same thing again soon. It was Manchester last night, it could be Liverpool tomorrow. The GWR expect our coaches to arrive in Exchange in twenty five minutes."

He nodded to them as he got up.

They finally pulled into Platform One at Northgate with the five coaches, and a small army of cleaners climbed in to begin the work of removing the blood, bandages and other evidence of the emergency use to which the coaches had been put. Jack looked across the tracks to Platform Two, where the morning businessmen and other commuters were waiting for their regular Manchester train.

"Look at that, Len," he commented, "Less than ten hours ago we watched a party of school kids, then we had the platform full of dead and injured, and now the workers going to their jobs!"

"Get used to it, Jack," answered the driver, shaking his head sadly, "In 1915 I was firing at Liverpool Central and we saw the same thing then. Often injured matelots from Navy warships or merchant sailors from torpedoed cargo vessels; it went on for three more years. It's now 1940, and I'm wondering how long this lot will bloody well go on for."

4 – Even old codgers cop it (November 1940)

It was a cold and wet early winter's evening when Harry Collins climbed down from the cab as his train waited on Platform Four in Chester's General Station. He was tall, dark haired and in his early twenties. Harry strolled across to stand next to one of the tall brick pillars which separated the platform from Number Three bay in the Great Western part of the station. A GW express from Paddington had arrived behind a Hall which had already uncoupled. A large Prairie 2-6-2 tank engine had just backed onto the other end ready to take the train back out on the last leg of its journey.

"'Ave I got time fer a smoke?" Harry called to his driver.

"Yeah, we're not due out for eight minutes," replied the driver in the cab, "But I'm putting a brew on, so be quick if you want to wet your whistle as well. The next stop's Rhyl but there won't be time for a brew there; you'd have to wait till Llandudno Junction."

Driver Jim Burke had got out the tea can and was placing it on the shovel before sliding the latter into the firebox to boil the water.

"OK, be right with you," Harry answered as he lit the small cigarette. Woodbines were thin and didn't have the taste he craved, but they had the advantage of being cheap and were sold in paper packs of five.

Harry leaned against the brick pillar and watched the young Great Western fireman from the Prairie climb down on to the track to couple up to the express. Waiting until the other fireman was back on the platform, Harry asked him, "You a Chester man?"

"That's right," Lance peered closely, "You're firing the Llandudno? 'Aven't seen you before."

"First time on this run, supposed to be learnin' the road but we're short staffed," said Harry.

"Nice run up the coast for you then," said the Western fireman, "Bet you're glad to be out of Manchester tonight."

"It was still quiet in Exchange when we left. They don't like coming over in the daytime. Still, Chester, eh? Quiet place. Yer lucky bugger. I bet the Luftwaffe doesn't come 'ere much. I don't suppose yer see much of 'em in this neck of the woods. I might ask fer a transfer; Chester's got an LMS shed. Where to now?"

"Hooton, Rock Ferry and Birken'ead."

"Birken'ead? An' 'ere's me thinkin' you was a lucky bugger on a quiet run! If yer not off ter Birken'ead, where else d'yer go?"

"Mostly on the up main to Wolverhampton, sometimes Birmingham."

"Blimey! D'yer go anywhere where the Luftwaffe doesn't come on visitin' days?"

A call came from the Western cab. "Oi! Come on Lance, you lazy hound! Check the gauges!"

"Gotta go," said Lance with a grin, "My mate'll ram me shovel up me arse, if I drop a plug. See yer!"

"Yeah, good luck tonight at Birken'ead!"

"Ta!"

Lance scrambled back into his cab and Harry heard what he took to be a stream of abuse from the Prairie cab. He stubbed out his fag end and climbed back into his own cab.

"Now, about that tea, Sir James?" he said to Jim.

Harry's driver pointed to the full mug standing on the firebox shelf.

"Any more of your bloody cheek and I'll see you get a wet back before Rhyl," he remarked, "It's me that's got the regulator, remember. Now, check the signals, we should have a clear line any minute now."

"Who's out first, us or the Birken'ead?"

"Should be the Birkenhead, but if you remember that you're supposed to be working, you can keep your eyes peeled for the signals!"

The Platform Three starter signal clunked down and Lance put down his shovel, walked behind his driver, and peered back down the train for the guard's green flag. The whistle sounded and the flag waved from the far end of the train.

Lance pulled his head inside and said, "We've got the 'right away'."

"Right," said driver George Denton, as he gently lifted the big regulator handle. The locomotive started to move with its seven coaches.

As they slowly moved past the LMS Black Five on Platform Four, Lance lifted his hand in greeting to Harry in the cab opposite. He looked back along the bay platform to see the Hall class 4-6-0 which had brought their train in from Wolverhampton backing after them. It would go to the turntable inside the big triangle for turning and then move to the GW shed for servicing before returning south to its home shed at Salop. They eased right over the GWR main route to the south and the LMS tracks to North Wales, then on to the Birkenhead line past the long Chester GW shed with its queue of engines lined up outside.

"Who's that in the cab with Jim Burke on the Llandudno?" asked George.

"His name's Harry something; he's on his first run up the North Wales coast."

"Bet he's glad to get away from Manchester," commented George, easing up the regulator as the train hurried under the Brook Lane Bridge.

"Wish we was gettin' away from Birken'ead, instead of rushin' towards it," grumbled Lance, "Bet the bloody Luftwaffe gives us a pastin' again tonight."

"Yeah, well at least we can get away again later; the poor devils who live and work there can't escape," said George, checking his watch and entering the details in the book kept in the shelf in the cab roof.

Birkenhead Woodside station was pitch dark and the air raid sirens were sounding as they pulled in.

"Wouldn't you know it!" muttered George as he eased the train to a stop, "The blighters knew we were coming in!"

The passengers hurried out of the train as the porters directed them into the nearby air raid shelter. George shut off steam and Lance set the vacuum brake before he turned the locomotive handbrake right down, locking it firmly.

The stationmaster called them from the platform, "Into the railwaymen's shelter, lads, quick as you like!"

An hour later, the 'all clear' sounded and George climbed back into their cab while Lance hurried along the track to uncouple the coaches. On Lance's call, George eased the engine forward across the points towards the buffer stops, waiting for the points to slide over to allow him to back onto the release road. Lance grabbed the handrail as the engine passed, swung himself up, and stood on the bottom step. As the engine slowly passed the front of the train, he dropped off again and walked over to the front coach, ready to couple the engine up again bunker-first for the return trip to Chester.

"We'll have to put the bag in at Hooton, Mr Denton," said Lance as they rounded the left hand curve out of Birkenhead, "I didn't get a chance at Woodside to top her up."

"Alright, remind me to pull up right at the water tank," said George, looking back at the reflections in the clouds of the fires behind them as they accelerated towards Rockferry, "Wonder who copped it this evening?"

Lance peered back over the boiler, "Looks like Wallasey and the Birkenhead docks again, poor buggers." He was very glad they were on the way home again; he opened the firebox and put half a dozen shovels full of coal around the fire. He checked the steam pressure and then as he leaned out round the bunker for the signals, he saw a huge blue flash dead ahead.

"Christ! Mr D., did you see that? Ease off, for God's sake; there might be something on the road!"

George glanced at his fireman without altering the regulator. "Lance, you dopey twerp, how many times have you done this trip? Don't you recognize the Mersey Railway electric's flashes? They're always bright in the dark and rain!"

"Oh, yeah, of course!" Lance said sheepishly, "Should've realized."

They stopped at Rockferry to pick up the Liverpool passengers from the Mersey Railway. At Hooton, Lance climbed on the right hand side tank, opened the filler lid, put the heavy rubber water hose in, and topped up the water.

"Should be right now for the rest of the shift," he said, back in the cab.

The run from Hooton was uneventful and they pulled in to Number Two bay at Chester General. As they moved slowly in, they noticed the big Star class 4-6-0 and four extra coaches waiting in Number One bay to be used to strengthen their train on its continued journey to Paddington.

Lance released the steam heating pipe and the vacuum brake popped as he undid it. Then he uncoupled the locomotive from the coaches. He informed George that they were free and George eased the engine forward, towards the big hydraulic buffers. More passengers boarded the train, and there was a gentle thump as the express locomotive with its extra coaches backed onto the other end of the train.

When, shortly after, the express pulled slowly out of the platform, the Prairie followed the Paddington train out as far as the platform starter signal then waited for the signals to show the points clear and to the right across the main station throat to the Chester GW shed. The sharp curves brought squeals of protest from the driving wheel flanges as they clanked into the shed; the foreman was waiting for them as they stopped under the coaling stage.

"All right, George?" he asked, "Much trouble at Birkenhead tonight?"

"Not really, Sid," answered George, "There was a raid

on, as you know. Apart from making us twenty minutes late out again, we had no problems. But will the Paddington be able to make up the lost time?"

"I put a Forty on in good nick, with Ted Simmons and his mate. They should be able to make up some of the time before they come off at Wolverhampton. After that, it's an Old Oak or Stafford Road problem, not ours."

The Forties, or Star class, were older four-cylinder express passenger engines, some of them more than thirty years old, but maintenance was not what it had been before the War. The cabs of the Forties were small and exposed when compared with those of later locomotives but the crews generally liked them because they were strong and fast.

"Ted knows his stuff and he doesn't like being late. He'll certainly do what he can; but the train's heavy today and he'll need to pull hard up Gresford Bank, but he'll be racing along south of Ruabon!" George commented.

An hour later, while George and Lance were enjoying a mug of tea in the railwaymen's canteen, Sid came over with a grin on his face.

"You're right about Ted Simmons, George," Sid said with a chuckle, "I was just talking to the signalman at Basford who said that the Paddington had just belted through like a racehorse with a wasp up its bum! Ted won't be too late in Salop!"

Two days later, George and Lance were waiting for the signal in the bay on the Birkenhead run again as the Llandudno train pulled in opposite them on Platform Four.

As Lance had already coupled on to the train and checked the gauges, he said to his mate, "I'll just nip across and say ''owdo' to Mr Burke and 'Arry."

"OK," replied George, "We've got seven more minutes yet."

Lance climbed down and strolled across the platform to the cab of the LMS North Wales train. "'Ow was your Llandudno trip the other day?" he asked Harry, who had noticed him and come over to the driver's side of the cab.

"No fun at all," Harry said, leaning out, "We got attacked by a Jerry just outside Abergele! Bastard tried to bomb us but missed!"

"What the 'ell was a Jerry bomber doing at Abergele? That's a seaside resort for retired old codgers."

"Yeah, an' we thought we was lucky gettin' away from Manchester! 'Nice quiet place, Llandudno', says our shed foreman at Patricroft, 'ye'll enjoy yerselves'. Anyway, 'ow was Birken'ead?"

"Bloody air raids most nights. My mum was pleased I'd joined the Great Western, when the war broke out. 'At least you'll not be fighting, Lancelot', she said; but I didn't expect to be gettin' bombs dropped on me 'ead."

"Can't work it out," said Lance to George, as they slowed down for a home signal at danger near Mollington on the way to Birkenhead, "Why would the down Llandudno get attacked at Abergele?"

"Think about it, young Lance; you're a pilot on a Dornier trying to bomb Harland and Wolf in Belfast docks and dodging the ack-ack all the time. Your bomb aimer tells you the bomb release mechanism is jammed and the bombs won't come out. What do you do?"

"You can't 'ang about, it's a bloody long way 'ome from Belfast, so you turn and piss off back an' 'ope the Hurricanes don't find you."

"And you try to land at your Luftwaffe base with a dicky bomb release mechanism and large bombs on board?" asked George.

"Er... well, if you put it like that."

"Yes, well if the pilot's as dopey as my fireman, he might. But any sensible pilot would try very hard to jettison his bombs on the way home; and if the bomb release problem's fixed, where else would you drop the bombs but on a nice fat juicy train underneath you?" asked George, lifting the regulator again as the signal lifted to the clear position.

"P'raps I should've joined the Army after all. Seems

safer."

"Mate of mine's in the Army based in Torquay," remarked George, "Only works once or twice a fortnight, the rest of the time he sits in his office and reads manuals."

"Blimey! In the Army?"

"Yes, captain too, *and* he gets bonus money for the time he works."

"Torquay, eh? Beach, bars and beautiful birds in bathing costumes? Sounds very nice - a real cushy job. What's 'e do, when 'e's called out?" Lance was suddenly very interested.

"He's a UXB expert."

"UXB?"

"He defuses unexploded bombs."

"Mmm... I think I might stay firin' with the Great Western, even in Birken'ead in twenty minutes."

"You might be wise - who knows, one day you might learn how to boil the water and keep the engine steaming; and in fifty years you might even become a Driver."

5 - Marty makes his mark (March 1941)

Sidney Thomson, shed foreman at Chester Great Western shed, was in his office looking through his crew lists for a crew to shunt an unexpected and lengthy freight which had arrived in the GW goods yard.

The train had to be broken up and portions sent to three different destinations. The matter was important and urgent, as it was a military train and contained a number of bombs loaded into 'shocvans', specially fitted to prevent damage to fragile goods. These vans' bodies were fitted with springing to allow them to slide along the top of the chassis, thus giving the contents some protection in the event of rough shunting. Sid wanted a careful and experienced crew who would know not to take any risks when sorting the various vans and wagons.

"Fred Leeming," he muttered to himself, as his eye ran down the list, "I should've thought of him straightaway; he's old and reliable."

Fred was in his mid sixties already and should have retired before the War. He'd been kept on because not only was he willing but he was also keen to keep working. He was a bachelor and had nobody to go home to at night.

Fred had been given charge of a local goods train to Saltney and was in the cab of a 22xx class 0-6-0 light mixed traffic loco, preparing it for duty, when the foreman called him.

"Fred, I need to change your duty. I want you to break up the freight which has just come in from Crewe. It's a bit of a tricky job, as you'll have to separate eight shocvans with munitions and take them as short goods to Hooton where the RAF will come and pick up the load."

Fred was a tall, friendly, good-natured man. He shrugged his shoulders, "Fine, Sid, no skin off my nose. Will I take my fireman, young Willy, with me?"

"No Fred, Willy's only just a Passed Cleaner. I want you

to take someone with some experience of handling hazardous freights. You've got Marty Smith; he's a competent bloke."

"Marty?" Fred was not pleased to hear that, "Haven't you got anyone else? Marty might be a good fireman, but he's a miserable bugger, always complaining about something."

"Sorry Fred, he's all I can spare today, and the matter is urgent. I've had the RAF on the phone already, wanting to know where their little presents to Hitler are."

Half an hour later, Fred and Marty were in the cab of a Pannier which had fortunately already been prepared for another duty.

"Who's our shunter, then?" Marty asked Fred.

"It's Mick Olroyd," answered Fred.

"Mick's a daft sod, we'll 'ave to be careful with 'im."

"I'm sure we'll manage."

"'An' I've 'ad better engines than this Pannier; its handbrake is sticky," Marty continued.

"You've plenty of experience, Marty, you'll cope."

"Do we get overtime for this job?"

"Overtime? Why?" Fred stared at Marty.

"We've been pulled off our reg'lar work to do this."

"But we're not doing overtime, we're just doing different work."

"Yeah, well, we should get danger money for this shunting lark. I bet Sid doesn't ask for danger money for us."

"For God's sake, Marty, give it a rest will you. Sid told me he put you with me because I need an experienced and capable fireman. I could have had my own fireman, Willy Wilson; he may not have your know-how but he doesn't complain all the bloody time. Now, make sure we have enough coal in the bunker to see us through the whole job up to Hooton and back."

They had to pull back the first four wagons containing coal and deposit them in the coal siding, and were about to move forward to pick another five general-purpose vans. Then Mick Olroyd, the shunter, stopped next to the cab and called up, "Fred, we could get the train broken more quickly, if we was to do a spot o' fly shunting."

Fred stared down at him for a moment and then said, "Tell me Mick, where do you live again?"

"Yer know dam' well where I live, Fred, why d'you ask?"

"You live in Black Diamond Street, your missus lives in Black Diamond Street and your kids live there too. It's right next to these sidings!"

Mick stared up with a puzzled face. "So?"

"Have you seen the eight shocvans on this train?"

"Course I 'ave, that's why we could fly shunt – they'll come to no 'arm."

Marty now leaned out of the cab next to Fred.

"Listen Mick, you stupid twat, if them schocvans aren't shunted proper, they could blow up; we'd all go to buggery and so would most of Black Diamond Street!"

"Why the 'ell would they blow up?" Mick was clearly puzzled.

"Mick," said Fred patiently, "What does it say on the side of the vans, eh? Go and have a look."

Mick walked down the train to see and came hurrying back. "Crikey! 'Munitions'... that means bombs an' stuff, dunnit?"

"Yes, so be bloody careful!"

Fly shunting was a practice whereby a shunter running alongside a rake of wagons or vans could uncouple them on the run. The driver would brake sharply, allowing the loose vehicles to run on. Once they had cleared the points, these could be switched and the remaining vans or wagons could then be guided into a neighbouring siding. It required very careful agreement on signals between the driver and a skilled shunter. It was both difficult and dangerous and was, in any case, banned. However, it was occasionally practised by experienced railwaymen as it saved time and allowed difficult jobs to be completed more easily and, it must be admitted, with some flair. But fly shunting with munitions trains was not practised by those in their right minds.

Marty went back to his side of the cab, giving Fred a meaningful stare, but refrained from saying 'I told you so'.

The rest of the shunt proceeded without problem. Mick stayed far from the shocvans until he had to uncouple them, which he did gingerly and with great respect. Fred pushed the eight shocvans into a nearby refuge to pick up the guard's van and to confer with the guard about the run up to Hooton. This was normally a simple twenty minute run on the Birkenhead line; here they would leave the vans to be unloaded by the RAF and bring the empty stock back to Chester to be marshalled into another freight for Crewe.

As the short goods made its way to the Birkenhead line, Fred pointed at the Chester GW engine shed. "The Germans are silly to bomb the stations, they should aim at the engine sheds if they want to hold up the traffic; if they destroyed that place there'd be hardly any trains in the northern part of the Wolverhampton division for months. Without crews and engines, nothing would run."

"Yeah, stations can be repaired quickly, but crew training and engine building takes much longer."

It seemed as if the atmosphere in the cab, previously somewhat frosty, had begun to thaw.

As they passed the little halt at Upton-by-Chester, Marty looked back at the signal box, and said, "Did you see that, Fred?"

"See what?"

"I thought I saw the bobby waving at us."

"Was he?"

"I'm not sure; it looked a bit like it."

"Well, he didn't stop us, so it can't have been anything to worry about."

Marty didn't answer; he was about to say that they ought to stop and examine the train. But they were heading towards Mollington and the distant signal was at 'danger', so he warned Fred, who unhappily eased the regulator down.

"Why would they slow a Special with urgent freight?" he growled.

"Hey up, Fred, the home's at danger too!"

"What?" Fred was shocked. "They've stopped us? What the hell are they playing at? Listen Marty, go the box and ask the bobby what's up; they can't stop us here – we've got priority over everything!"

As the engine slowed down, Marty climbed down the steps. He was about to drop off onto the ballast when he looked back at the train. He saw smoke coming from low down on one of the shocvans.

"Fred!" he called urgently, "We've got a hot box on one of the vans!"

"Christ almighty, and us with a munitions train! Is the guard signalling at all?"

"Can't see 'im, I bet 'e doesn't know anything's wrong!"

"Well he should be trying to find out why we've stopped! Go and see what he's doing, Marty, but take care!"

Marty dropped down to the track and ran back to where he could see smoke. There was no doubt; an axle box on the last of the munitions vans was smoking, but there were no flames as yet.

The guard was between the vans, uncoupling the smoking van from the rest of the train. "Marty!" he shouted, "Get Fred to move away with the rest of the train while I run back with some detonators to stop anything coming on the up line!"

"Have you got any water in your van to cool off the axle box?"

"Jeez, I have at that! Go an' get some, but for God's sake get the rest of the train out of danger!"

Marty grabbed the kettle and the full water bucket from the guard's van and tipped the water over the axle box, which sizzled furiously. Then, seeing as the guard had uncoupled the van with the hot box, he raced back to the engine to tell Fred to pull the rest of the vans away to safety. In the cab he found Fred lying on the cab floor.

Seizing Fred's shoulders, he pulled him out of the way, and, grabbing the regulator, tried to raise it, but first it stuck and then abruptly moved and the engine responded slowly at first, then with increasing speed.

When Marty had drawn the train about a half a mile away to relative safety, he slowed and stopped it. He went over to where Fred was lying and shook his shoulder gently.

"Fred! Are you OK, mate?" The driver groaned but didn't move. There was blood running down his face from a cut on his forehead. Marty tried to make him comfortable and then climbed down from the cab to warn the signalman what had happened.

The signalman in the cabin, known as the 'bobby' to railwaymen, was waiting for him; he had already been in contact with the bobby at Upton-by-Chester who thought he had seen a hot box as the train passed.

"I've been on to Hooton," the Mollington bobby said, "You're to take the train on there as quick as you can. The line's cleared for you; we've got the Army Bomb Disposal unit from the Dale Barracks at Upton already with your burning van, so you can leave it to them."

"Right, ta, I'll get back to the rest of the train, then," said Marty without telling the bobby about his driver's incapacity; he didn't want to waste any time with questions and decisions.

Back in the cab, he unwound the brake and eased the regulator, taking the train at a steady pace through Capenhurst and into the goods yard at Hooton, where several heavy RAF lorries were waiting.

Leaning out of the cab, he called out, "Any doctor about? I've got an injured driver here!"

Within a few minutes, medical help had arrived and Fred was gently lifted out of the cab, placed on a stretcher and carried over to a blue RAF ambulance.

"Don't worry, mate, we'll look after 'im," said the RAF driver, "We'll let the stationmaster 'ere at 'Ooton know when 'e can be collected."

Nodding his thanks, Marty went back to the

40

stationmaster to report the details.

"Are you the fireman?" asked the stationmaster, after Marty had explained what had happened to his driver.

"Of course," answered Marty, very shaken and tired by this time.

"You aren't allowed to drive any train, let alone a munitions train!" said the stationmaster angrily, "This is a serious business; I'll have to report it. You even drove the train without a guard and guard's van!"

"Yes," answered Marty, "I know; next time I'll wait for a qualified driver..."

"Right, you..."

"... And let the whole train blow up. Save us all a lot of trouble," Marty continued.

"You can't talk to me like that! I'm a stationmaster!" shouted the stationmaster in a fury.

"You're also a bloody fool," replied Marty, angry himself by now, "What did you expect me to do?"

"I'll be on to your shed foreman Sid Thomson about your attitude! I'll have you sacked!"

"You do that," answered Marty, and he stalked away.

"What do you think had happened to Fred?" asked Sid Thomson when Marty reported back to him later that day.

"I don't know, but the RAF medics seemed to think he wasn't badly hurt; they said he'd be sent back to us when he was OK."

"Mmmm," replied Sid, "I also understand you weren't happy with the Hooton stationmaster; he was on the phone to me an hour ago."

"Sorry about that, Sid, I got a bit hot under the collar with him."

"Don't worry about it; the man's been a pain in the arse for years. God knows why he was made up to stationmaster. I told him that you and the guard deserve medals for what you both did, and if there's any sacking to be done, he'd be at the top on my list."

As Sid was speaking, his phone rang. He picked it up, listened, then said, "Thanks very much for that, we'll keep an eye on him," and hung up. "That was RAF Hooton; they've cleaned up Fred and put him on the Oswestry for us to pick him up here. They said something about him breaking his hand on his face. What the hell could they mean?"

Marty frowned, and then suddenly grinned.

"I think I know," he said, "I noticed that the Pannier's handbrake was sticky. I bet the lever jerked, hit his face, and knocked him cold."

"Yes, well it obviously hasn't done any permanent damage. Now Marty," Sid said, "As a Passed Fireman, I think it's about time you went for your Driver's test. We're badly short of competent blokes."

6 - Lance goes to prison (May 1941)

In Wolverhampton, when George Denton and Lance Hargreaves took their Castle into the shed for servicing after an uneventful run from Chester on the Birkenhead to the south coast express, the Stafford Road shed foreman was standing outside his office looking worried.

"Looks like trouble for someone, Mr Denton," commented Lance as they left the engine and walked towards the crew canteen.

"Well, I'll be buggered! George Denton! How are ye, George?" The voice came down from the cab of a Pannier being readied for a shift.

George looked up to see an older driver leaning out of the cab; his hair was greying and his face had a reddish hue which emphasized the broad smile over it.

"Dean!" George grinned. "Dean Stephens! Haven't seen you in years, mate. How's life?" He turned to his fireman, "Dean was my driver when I worked at Bristol, St Phillip's Marsh."

Dean climbed down from the cab of the Pannier and he shook hands with his ex-fireman.

"It's good to see you, Dean!" said George, "How's the missus? And how's that good-looking daughter of yours?"

Dean's face darkened. "We've had some bad luck," he answered, "Mary married a very nice bloke, a Lieutenant in the Navy, but the poor devil didn't come back from Dunkirk. She's left with two young kids to look after. Dianne and I help of course, but I'm not home much, as you know, being a railwayman."

"I'm really sorry to hear that, Dean, but look on the bright side, he might be a prisoner."

"No, his captain said he was in a landing party which got caught by the Jerries. We heard from the Red Cross. The Germans gave them a list of names of the dead they could identify," Dean shrugged, "His was one of the names.

43

We've just got to live with it. Mary's a nurse now and her work helps; and the kids are at school."

George nodded, "Yeah, it can be hard; we've been lucky so far, we've only lost a distant cousin."

"Anyway," said Dean, "Where are you based now, since you moved from St Phillip's Marsh after you became a Driver? I heard you'd gone to Salop."

"Only for a few months, I moved again to Chester."

As they stood outside the Pannier cab chatting, the shed foreman came up to them: "You two the Chester crew off the Margate?"

"That's right," answered George.

"And I hear you're an ex-St Phillip's Marsh man?"

"Right again," said George suspiciously, "Why?"

"You might know the road to Bristol from here then?"

George's heart sank. He knew what was coming and put up a quick objection, "I do, but Lance here doesn't."

"Sorry about this, but I can't do anything else, I'm stuck with a special to Bristol and it's urgent. I need a crew to take it, and I've got nobody left here who knows the road."

"What sort of special?"

"It's a troop train - eight 35-tonners; you'll get a clear run most of the way, and I'll give you my best Forty."

George sighed, "OK, we'll take it." He turned to his fireman, "Sorry Lance, I hope you didn't have anything planned for later."

"Good lads. I'll let Sid know in Chester, that you've been requisitioned. He can't complain - he did the same thing to me three months ago. Now, grab a mug of tea, the engine's ready and you're due out in twenty-five minutes."

George turned back to his old driver. "Dean, I hope we can catch up again, we're often in Stafford Road."

Early next morning, George and Lance were returning to Chester, having taken their special to Bristol. The Bristol shed foreman had been very thankful to see their train and organized a hostel for them overnight before finding them an easy duty taking a slow goods to Hereford on their way back home.

They were held up in a small refuge a few miles outside Hereford. George took the opportunity to have a brew up as he expected them to be held in the refuge for at least half an hour.

"I'm just going to stretch my legs, Mr D.," said Lance, and he climbed down from the cab of the old twenty-eight class goods engine.

"Tea'll be ready in two minutes!" warned George.

"Be right back!"

A few minutes later, Lance returned; he had a puzzled frown on his face. "Where are we?" he asked.

"A few miles south east of Hereford," replied George, "Why?"

"I've just been to the end of this refuge and there's another set of points with a track leading round a curve. Where's it go to?"

"Oh, that; it leads to an old, disused quarry. Hasn't been used for years. Now, get the tea down your neck while it's still hot."

"Something funny about the points though," said Lance, sipping his tea, "I stepped on the rusty track and my foot slipped off it. That track's been used recently; it's shiny, but someone has put brown paint on it to make it look rusty."

At that moment, the signal clanged and the points switched over, clearing their way back onto the main line.

"Never mind about brown paint, my lad, get shovelling - we're off again!"

The Hereford shed foreman arranged for them to return to Chester via Shrewsbury 'on the cushions', in a first class coach in some comfort, as thanks for their long extra shift.

"Anyone seen Lance Hargreaves, my fireman?" George called out in the engine crew cabin next day. Their shift was about to begin and Lance hadn't shown up. There was a card game around the scarred table, several other crewmen were eating their sandwiches and three were dozing semi-upright on the long bench.

Just then, Sidney Thomson, the shed foreman, came in. "George, I need to speak to you, come outside for a minute, will you?"

Outside, Sid took his hat off - a worrying sign, thought George.

"George, what the hell has young Hargreaves been up to under your care?"

"What d'you mean, what's he been up to? Where is he?"

"He's in the hands of military security people in an army base. He's been accused of espionage!"

"*Espionage*? Look, Sid, Lance is going to be a good fireman and he's a bright spark too, but he left school at fourteen and didn't finish his education. He couldn't even spell espionage."

"He's been accused of spying near Hereford. You were both at Hereford last week."

"Of course we were. We were taking a slow goods from Bristol to Hereford. Lance was with me all the time in the cab. What army base anyway?"

"I don't bloody know," Sid was clearly annoyed that one of his people had been accused of such unpatriotic activities, "He was with you all the time? In the cab? He never left the cab?"

"He only popped out to stretch his legs. We were waiting in a refuge; he was back in the cab inside two minutes!"

"What else did he do there?"

"I was brewing up, I wasn't watching him. But I recall he was a bit puzzled when he came back, he said - er - something about the old quarry there."

"What did you do then?"

"We got the clear from the signal and moved off."

"Is that all he did?"

"He didn't have time to do anything else."

"Well, we won't be seeing him for a while. He's in clink."

"That's damned ridiculous! The lad's still young and

keen on the railways; he loves the job, he wouldn't do anything stupid like spying. He's got a good family, he's good-natured, although he's a lecherous young devil, I'll grant you that; anything in a skirt is a target. But *spying*? Never!"

"Yeah, well that's pretty much what I told the Colonel. He's waiting to speak to you in my office now."

Inside Sid's office a tall, dignified man with a military bearing was waiting. Sid and George entered and the man stood up.

"I'm Colonel Hannigan," he said to George "And I'd like to ask you a few questions about your fireman, Lance Hargreaves."

"Do you need me here, too?" asked Sid of the colonel.

"No, I really need to conduct the interview in private; thank you, Mr Thomson."

"Right, I'll leave you to it. But can I have my driver in half an hour? He's on duty."

"I hope so," nodded the colonel, who sat down and requested George to do the same.

"Now, Mr Denton, can you tell me exactly what happened when your train was held in the siding near Hereford last Wednesday?"

George told him what he had just told the foreman but added the bit about the painted rails, which he had omitted to mention to the foreman.

"And what did you say to your fireman, when he told you about the painted rails?"

"As he climbed back into the cab, the signal cleared and I told him to get shovelling as we had to move. I also told him he was dreaming. We'd had a very long shift the previous day."

"And did he pursue the topic with you?"

"No."

"What do *you* think he saw?"

"I know what he saw. The rails *had* been painted."

The colonel stiffened and asked coldly, "Could you explain what you mean?"

"I used to drive in the Bristol division," explained

47

George, "And I often made that run to Hereford. Late one night three or four years back, we had to wait in that refuge, and my then fireman got caught short and disappeared into some bushes. While we were waiting there, a Pannier with a very short goods came past. It moved over the points, past my train and into the curve to the old quarry. I was going to tell my fireman of the curious matter when I saw a soldier come out of an old tracklayer's shack and start to paint the rails. I realized then that it was something the Army didn't want talked about."

"Did your fireman see this train at the time?"

"No, and he didn't hear it either. He was desperate and had a touch of diarrhoea. He was more concerned with his stomach."

"And have you ever discussed what you saw with anyone else?"

"No."

"Not your wife or your family?"

"Nobody."

The colonel suddenly changed tack. "Why did you leave the army in 1919, Mr Denton? You were offered a promotion to sergeant; a very rare distinction for a corporal immediately after the war, when thousands were being demobbed."

George was staggered. "How the devil did you know that?"

"Just answer the question, please."

George shrugged. "It was nothing against the Army, but railways are in the family. My dad and granddad were both with the Great Western, and I wanted to be a driver too."

"Do you regret your choice of career now?"

"Only when the Jerries try to plaster us with their bombs."

The colonel got up and paced up and down for a few moments before turning to George: "I trust you will forget all that we have discussed; you would be doing the country a very great favour."

"I know when to keep my trap shut."

"Yes," said the colonel thoughtfully, "I believe you do. One more thing: if you should overhear any further talk about that quarry - any mention at all - please contact Major Smithers at Western Command here in Chester instantly. He will get in touch with me."

"Major Smithers; yes, I'll do that."

"I'm much obliged to you; oh and I'll have your fireman sent back; we will tell him he's been arrested in error - a question of mistaken identity. We might even give him some compensation payment."

"Where the hell have you been these last few days, Lance?" George greeted his fireman two days later as Lance walked into the GW shed for duty.

"Wait!" he said, putting his hand up as Lance began to speak, "Don't tell me; let me guess. Her father or husband found out and you had to disappear. You decided three days' loss of pay was better than a week in hospital?"

"No, nothing like that. I've been..." Lance was not his usual ebullient self; he lowered his voice, "I've been in prison."

"You've been...?"

"Shhh! Not so loud! It was all a mistake - they said they'd got the wrong bloke and were very sorry. I also got a few bob compensation, but I'll tell you, Mr Denton, I got the fright of me life in there. They thought I was a spy."

"You? A spy? My God, they *did* make a mistake, didn't they?"

"Yeah but listen," Lance breathed, "Don't tell the blokes - I'd never live it down!"

"Well now," considered George, "If I were to get a free pint at The Wheatsheaf once a week for the next month, I dare say this could damage my memory."

"You're on!" said Lance gratefully, "I'll even make it two pints."

"Not on your wages, lad," replied George, "One pint's fine. Now, we've got an engine to prepare. We've got an old 43 class 2-6-0 on a loose coupled goods down to Corwen, and we return on the Pwllheli-Birkenhead semi-fast. It's a long and hilly duty and should take your mind off things as you'll be shovelling hard there and back!"

The old engine had seen many better days and was well overdue for a 'sole and heel' or a light repair, but owing to wartime demands, engines were often kept on duty long after they needed maintenance. Consequently, their goods engine steamed poorly, the glands leaked and it generally kept both crewmen fully occupied. The climb up Gresford Bank was particularly hard and they had to set back into a refuge on the bank to let an express passenger past and to allow the engine to build up enough steam pressure again. They didn't get much chance to admire the beautiful scenery in the charming run through Llangollen and the stretch of railway through the Dee Valley.

At Corwen they thankfully booked off and handed over to the relief crew from Bala.

"She'll keep you both busy - she needs looking after!" said George to the relief driver.

"Don't worry, boyo!" said the Welshman cheerily, "We know her well, she's one of ours and we know how to tickle her up!"

The two Chester men went over to the railwaymen's cabin for a mug of tea and their cheese sandwiches.

"You did well today, Lance," commented George, "That was a hard run with the old lady. We might be lucky and get something better on the Birkenhead and you won't have to bend your back so much through the hills."

Lance was exhausted. "Thank God for that," he replied, "I could do with a nice rest. We must've used a ton of coal more than we should 'ave. What d'yer think we'll get from Pwllheli?"

"Could be a Manor, if we're lucky. The new light 4-6-0s are said to be ideal for light passenger trains in hilly areas. But I've not driven one yet."

An hour later their train from Pwllheli to Birkenhead

pulled in and George was delighted to see a Manor at the head.

"We're in luck, Lance," he said, "We've got a Manor to look after. Let's hope it's as good as they say."

But George and Lance were not in luck; the Pwllheli crew were glad to get off it.

"I'd rather have an old 43," said the driver, "At least you expect to be short of steam. These engines are new and supposed to be much better, but they're bloody not!"

By the time George and Lance had reached Ruabon where they joined the main line to the north, they had to agree with the Welsh crew. The Manor was shy of steam, and Lance had had to bend his back to keep up the steam pressure; consequently, he hadn't been able to relax through the winding valley of the Dee. The only place where he was able to sit down for a few minutes was down Gresford Bank and across the Dee plain to Saltney. George took pity on him and took the shovel and fired through Saltney Junction to the Curzon Park cutting. Then they could let the fire down through the Chester tunnels and into Number Three bay, where a Prairie with a Birkenhead crew took over the train.

As they walked over the long footbridge to the Hoole Road entrance and down the steps to the GWR shed, Lance said, "I'm glad I didn't have to stay in clink, Mr D. Just think o' years o' hard labour like today!"

"No hard labour for spies, young Lance!"

"No? What then? Sewin' mailbags?"

"You wouldn't be sewing mailbags either."

"Sounds like an easy life! Yer sit around doin' nothin' and get all meals free."

"I suppose you could say it's an easy life, but I wouldn't recommend it."

"Why's that then?"

"Spies are hanged!"

"Blimey! I'll 'ave ter watch meself in future!"

7 - The pilot (August 1941)

The clear blue early morning sky over Whitchurch railway station was suddenly disturbed by the staccato rattle of multiple machine gun fire. Two low-flying Junkers JU 88s heading south had been caught by a lone Spitfire, and the aircraft were exchanging fire.

"Hey, look at that, Steve!"

Engine driver Harry Percival pointed into the sky as he and his fireman were waiting in the platform with a York to Bristol semi-fast train.

While the engine was stationary, fireman Steve duCane was taking the opportunity to shovel more coal into the firebox of the Black Five. He looked up to see what his driver was staring at; one of the German bombers was in serious trouble, with one engine streaming smoke. The Spitfire had just strafed it and was circling round to attack again, but it had also been hit, by the gunner in the other bomber.

Harry and Steve heard the British plane's engine splutter and cough, then part of its tailplane fell off. The cheers from the waiting passengers on the platform fell silent as the Spitfire tried to climb and then stalled. They all saw the cockpit cover slide back and the pilot jump out, and the cheers broke out again as his parachute opened.

In the meantime, the stricken German bomber flew on, smoke still billowing from its engines. Two figures could be seen in the distance, baling out of the aircraft. The second bomber began to climb steeply and disappeared into clouds.

"Them Jerry aircrew in parachutes won't get far," commented Steve, "The army'll 'ave 'em before yer can say 'Jack Robinson'."

"There's an RAF Station at Shawbury not far away, and another at Tern Hill; they might even be able to nail the other bomber if that Spit pilot has radioed in," replied Harry.

"'Ang on, Mr Percival!" called Steve; he was watching for the guard's green flag for the 'off', when he saw the Spitfire pilot drifting down with the wind towards the station, "That pilot's driftin' this way!"

The station staff had also apparently seen the pilot, and the burly figure of a local bobby on his bike could be seen hurriedly pedalling down the road to the station. In the meantime, the pilot had landed on the railway tracks just outside the station. He was rolling up the parachute when he was met by two station porters who escorted him onto the platform and towards the stationmaster's office.

"Funny!" said one porter to Harry Percival as they walked past the Black Five cab, "'E don't sound like one of our pilots!"

"Why?"

"Well, listen to 'im."

By this time, several of the passengers had gathered round and were listening. The pilot's face showed a streak of blood down one side and he was trying to explain something.

"I mus' back to RAF station Shawbry! Quick! More German aircraft! Zey come!" he said.

A small man in a cloth cap standing by and listening shouted, "'E's not RAF, 'e's a bloody Jerry! 'E baled out o' that bomber! Let's scrag the bugger!"

A number of other passengers murmured approval.

Harry barged his way in front of the excited passenger and pushed the man back.

"Wait a minute before you do something daft," he said and called up to his fireman who had been watching. "Steve, you saw him, is this bloke the Spitfire pilot or a German airman?"

"It's the Spit pilot; I watched 'im come down."

"There you go," Harry said to the angry passenger, "He's RAF, you dozy get! Now let him be."

But the passenger was not to be put off: "Then why don't 'e speak like an RAF pilot? All posh-like, eh?"

The pilot turned to the man and shouted at him. "I RAF pilot! Polski Flight!"

Harry took the pilot's arm gently. "You'll be OK, mate, we'll look after you."

He opened the pilot's jacket and showed the upper shoulder flash to the doubting passenger; "Look at that – one blue stripe – he's Polish and a Flying Officer in our Air Force, now leave him alone."

"I still think 'e's a bloody Jerry in disguise. I say we thump 'im 'ere and now!"

"Nobody's doing any thumping on my patch!" The elderly bobby had arrived puffing and pushed the passenger away, "You clear off, or I'll arrest you for causing a breach of the peace!"

"Listen, Constable," Harry pointed to the cab of his engine, "We're due in Wem next stop; we can have him there in fifteen minutes where RAF Shawbury can pick him up. It'd be much quicker than getting them to send a van out here. You can phone them and then get the MPs to catch the Jerry airmen."

"Well," said the bobby doubtfully, "But you can't leave him on his own in the train; some of the passengers might misunderstand and silly things could happen."

"He won't be in a coach, we'll keep him here in the cab with us; he'll be OK for twenty minutes."

"Well, if you're sure. But won't you have to clear it with your bosses?"

"Control won't mind," said Harry airily, "Especially if they don't know."

As they pulled into Wem, the Polish pilot, looking out of the cab behind Harry Percival, pointed to the platform and said excitedly, "Zere! RAF officers! Zey come for me!"

A pair of men in RAF uniforms stood watching as the train came in.

One of them, smiling, called out as the slowing engine passed him, "Bad luck Hendrik, but we've got a Hurricane for you if you're OK!"

54

The second man looked more serious.

"Zat is good fren' Nick!" the pilot said proudly to the cab crew, then he frowned, "But ozzer man is Flight Lieutenant; he is boss. He ask hard question! Why I lose Spit!"

The two officers moved to the cab as the train stopped. The younger one shook the pilot's hand, asking, "Are you really OK? Not hurt at all?"

The senior one addressed the engine crew, "We'd like to thank you lads for bringing our pilot so quickly to us; Hendrik is one of our best pilots. He's knocked out three enemy fighters already this year, so we can't afford to lose him. If you give us your names, we'll make sure the LMS knows about the assistance you've given us today."

"No need to mention it at all to anyone," said Harry quickly, "Your Polish bloke knocked out a German bomber and the crew have probably been caught by now so they can't do us any more damage."

"Yes," replied the Flight Lieutenant, "The JU 88 crashed and one of our Hurricanes caught the other one, but without Hendrik here, both German bomber aircrews might have got away, so that's two more we don't have to worry about."

Hendrik thanked them again as he moved off with his two RAF colleagues, and Harry and Steve took their train on south to Shrewsbury, where Harry sent Steve down to uncouple the engine. A GWR Castle 4-6-0 was waiting to couple up and haul the train on to Bristol, while they would take their Black Five to the LMS shed at Coleham for turning and servicing before returning to the station to pick up a Bristol-to-Manchester express.

On their way to the shed, Harry commented to his fireman, "I hope to God they don't tell anyone at Crewe. Control'd have our balls for breakfast if they thought we'd had a foreigner in the cab without permission!"

Harry Percival walked into the crew cabin at Crewe North with some interesting news a week later.

"Hey-up, young Steve, you're in for a treat!" he called

as he came in, "They've given us a big engine to play with; it's in great nick, just out of the works for repair and we're taking it to Salop and back for a running-in turn!"

"What is it?"

"It's a streamliner, number 6239, now you'll see what the top link men get."

"We're getting a Pacific on the Shrewsbury semi-fast?" Steve asked in surprise.

"Yep, we run her down to Salop, turn her on the table, service her and run her back here. We have to report anything we think still needs looking at."

Harry was rubbing his hands in glee; in his late thirties, he was a relatively young driver and hadn't often been able to get his hands on the big LMS Pacifics.

Crewe North shed had several of the big Princess and Duchess 4-6-2s for the top link London, Glasgow and Liverpool turns, but they were rarely used on other duties. Yet when Steve saw the huge bulbous shape of the streamlined smoke-box front and the immensely long boiler cladding, he was disappointed.

"It's not very clean," he grumbled, looking at the grimy red of the engine with the yellow lines along the boiler barely discernible under the dirt.

"Clean?" replied his driver, checking the contents of his oilcan, "You want jam on it as well! Listen, they don't waste too much time cleaning these days; clean engines are for peacetime. We're damn lucky to get one straight out of the Works! Now hop up and check the handbrake's hard on, while I oil the inside motion."

When a driver was oiling the inside motion he was usually hard up against the huge steel counterweights on the crank axle; if the engine moved even half an inch, the swing of the counterweights could easily crush him to death. It had happened.

There were only six corridors on the Shrewsbury train, but even so, Steve was astounded feeling the sheer power of the big engine as Harry took the train southwards and to the right, past the Crewe South sheds with smoke and steam from the dozens of goods engines, and on to the Shrewsbury and Hereford line.

"She's pulling as if there weren't any coaches on," he commented to his driver.

"Yeah, six coaches is nothing for this engine, she's more used to hauling sixteen at seventy or eighty miles an hour, and what's more, taking them over Tebay and Shap without assistance," answered Harry, clearly enjoying himself immensely, "But young Steve, you'd better get shovelling; this isn't a little tankie or a Black Five. These Pacifics have huge, greedy fireboxes. By the time you get home, you'll have some very sore muscles!"

In spite of his enthusiasm though, Harry wasn't entirely happy with the performance and reported a stickiness in the regulator lever and an unusual 'clunk' from the left-hand coupling rod, which the Salop fitter temporarily eased but couldn't cure. These issues were duly noted and the engine went back into the Works.

Two days later, Harry and Steve were asked to take the locomotive out again and compare its performance with its previous duty; this time they were given an Empty Coaching Stock train to Chester; a mere half hour's run. ECS trains were not advertised to the public and did not take passengers.

The faults had obviously been corrected as the engine ran well and pulled into Chester General Number Six bay right on time. As Steve climbed out of the cab to uncouple, he noticed an RAF officer walking past who must have somehow got into the empty train at Crewe.

He recognized him and called to his driver, "Hey Mr Percival, here's Hendrik, that Polish bloke we gave a lift to a fortnight ago; we've apparently given 'im a lift again."

Harry came over and leaned out of the cab to see them. "Blimey, so it is! How are you, Hendrik? All OK after your little argument with the Luftwaffe?"

Hendrik came over, nodded and smiled. "Yes, I fine. I have Hurricane now. Very strong plane."

"What are you doing here? I thought you were at Shawbury."

"Yes, Shawbury is base, but I visit brother in hospital."

"What hospital?"

"Here – Chester Royal Infirmary!"

"You were bloody lucky to catch this particular train. It's empty coaches – doesn't take passengers."

"Not lucky – train say 'Chester'."

Harry was puzzled, "No, this train isn't on the public timetable – the notice in Crewe didn't announce it as a Chester train!"

"Yes – it say 'Chester' on train."

Harry looked at his fireman. "What the devil's he talking about? We're ECS – we're only running in to check the faults have been fixed; how did he know the empty coaches were for Chester?"

Steve shook his head. "Search me, but 'e seems sure about it."

Harry spoke to the pilot again. "Hendrik, where does it say 'Chester' on this train?"

The Pole pointed to the metal nameplate along the engine's boiler: "There! It say *City of Chester*!"

Harry and Steve hooted with laughter.

"I 'ope yer luck stays with yer right through the War, yer jammy sod!" laughed Steve, shaking the puzzled Hendrik by the hand.

"And give your brother our best wishes," added Harry.

8 - The job's no doddle (February 1942)

"I always like driving these engines," commented Fred Leeming to his fireman Willy Wilson as they climbed aboard the big 47xx class 2-8-0.

In this he agreed with most of the men who crewed them. The nine engines in the class had been built by G. J. Churchward in 1919. Designed for heavy, fast freight traffic, they were Churchward's final design, and were occasionally used for heavy relief passenger trains as well.

Fred and Willy were relieving the Oxley crew at Wolverhampton to take the Acton to Birkenhead freight, known to railwaymen as the 'Northern Flier', for the final leg of its journey to Birkenhead docks.

Fred's comment to his fireman was overheard by the Oxley driver as he lifted his lunchbox from the tender tool shelf.

"Well, you won't like this one, Fred. She's got a leaky right cylinder and we didn't get time to empty the smokebox properly before we took her out. Mind you," the local driver added, "There was a raid on Acton yard just as we came on shift and we had to leave a bit sharpish like."

"Thanks for the warning," replied Fred, "We'll have to see what we can do."

He turned to his fireman, "You're going to have your work cut out, Willy. It sounds like we're in for a hard time on this trip."

Fred took the train gently out of Oxley yard, feeling for the problems the Oxley driver had mentioned.

Willy looked at the gauge glass then examined the fire. He opened the flap to the firebox and looked inside.

"Mmm," he said, shaking his head, "It doesn't look too good."

Fred also looked in and said, "Get the pricker and give the fire a good pull through before you start firing."

Willy levered the long pricker from the tender and twisted it round to slide it into the firebox. The pricker was a steel shaft about twelve feet long with a hook at the far end; it was used to rake the fire and break up any clinker building up.

"Watch out, Willy!" called Fred urgently, "Mind the signal post!"

Willy, warned by his driver's shout, was able to jerk the pricker back, but the end still caught on a signal post they were passing and the jolt almost broke Willy's arm. Fortunately, he held on to the shaft grimly in spite of the pain, and was able to slide it into the firebox.

"Willy!" growled Fred, "Always watch for passing obstructions when you're lifting the fire irons. Ten years ago a fireman with me lost his arm when the pricker caught on the side of a bridge we were passing. It crushed his arm on the cab side."

"Thanks for the warning; I won't make that mistake again," said Willy gratefully and rubbed his right arm. He had been shocked by the sudden danger. He then flattened out the fire with the pricker, filling in some of the holes before he started to fire again. Looking at the tender, he was dismayed to see that although it had been filled with coal, many of the lumps were far too big to fit into the firehole. He would have to spend a lot of time on the tender just breaking them up.

"I'll give you a hand from time to time, this run's going to be rough even for an experienced fireman, and for a Passed Cleaner it'll be doubly tricky."

Enginemen began their careers as cleaners and were promoted to 'Passed Cleaner' when the powers that be felt they could be trusted to handle limited firing duties with an experienced driver.

Further promotion to 'Fireman' and later to 'Driver' came through formal and practical exams and took many years. During wartime, however, the time spent in moving up to Driver was shortened of necessity.

Firemen had one point in their favour: they were usually fit. When you had to shovel four tons of coal into a

60

firebox in the course of day's work, you either stayed fit or left the cab. The job was physically hard and very dirty, and demanded far more skill than the firemen were normally given credit for. It could also be dangerous, quite aside from the attentions of enemy aircraft.

More than one fireman had been killed by being hit by a bridge as he stood on the tender having to break up large lumps of coal, or by simply lifting one of the long fire irons from their casing in the tender to slide into the firebox. And you could hear a word or two from your driver when you pulled out a pricker with a red hot end and just missed his leg as you swung it back into the tender casing. Cramped cabs weren't the best places to wave twelve-foot pieces of steel around.

They managed with some difficulty as far as Shrewsbury, but after Baschurch Willy had to work hard to keep up the steam pressure. No matter how hard he shovelled and worked the injectors, pressure kept dropping. As they crawled past the Ruabon signal box, Fred called to the train's bobby to pass a message to the Wrexham bobby, to let them into a loop so they could stop and build up steam. A wave from the box indicated that the message had been received and would be passed on.

"I'm not even sure we'll make Wrexham," muttered an exhausted Willy as he watched the pressure gauge dropping again. Willy had shovelled almost two tons of coal into the firebox since Wolverhampton. He was black with coal dust and sweat, and his arm was still very sore from the injury with the pricker.

"Willy, take the weight off your feet for a few minutes and sit down. Let me put a few in," said Fred and he took the shovel and put a dozen shovelfuls around the firebox, then four more down the front. The engine slowly picked up speed, but they were nevertheless relieved to see the signal at Wrexham guiding them into the loop. There was a fitter from the Wrexham shed at Croes Newydd waiting for them and he watched as they trundled into the loop.

"I can pack the right cylinder gland for you to get you to

Birkenhead, but it'll be very temporary," he commented, "And I can't guarantee it'll hold. You might need to stop in Chester and change engines."

As they were speaking, an express passenger passed them, picking up speed after stopping at the station. It was hauled by an elderly Bulldog class 4-4-0. Its outside frames reminded one of the heavy armour on a tank but, ancient although she was, 3442 *Bullfinch* was running well with only a wisp of smoke emanating from the chimney and its great, protruding coupling rods whisking smoothly round and round.

"Look at that!" chuckled Fred as the express passed, "Those engines are nearly forty years old and should have been scrapped years ago, but they've still got plenty of life in them."

Willy got busy with his shovel again, after passing an envious glance at the Bulldog, and Fred showed him where best in the firebox to throw the coal. Finally, when the pressure gauge showed enough to get them going, they whistled and the signal fell, allowing them to move slowly out on to the main line again.

"Well at least we're downhill from here to Balderton, Willy, and then there's the straight stretch to build up a bit of speed to get up to Saltney Junction, then it's pretty flat to Chester."

"Are we going to stop there and change engines, Mr Leeming?"

"Let's see how we're going when we get there; we're routed to bypass Chester straight on to the Birkenhead road, but if she's not performing well, we might have to stop and get assistance or even change engines. We'll see."

The work of the Croes Newydd fitter seemed to have been satisfactory as the engine steamed well enough to take them through Saltney and on the triangle past the Chester turntable and shed, straight onto the Birkenhead line. There were no tricky grades between Chester and Birkenhead and Fred decided to risk taking the big 47xx class through to the docks.

The whole trip was for Willy a very useful learning experience as Fred showed him some of the tricks he had learned in his long footplate career as to how to get the best out of a poor steaming locomotive.

Both enginemen were looking forward to their break and a cup of tea as they pulled into the docks, when the air raid warning sounded. Since they had just stopped in the siding for unloading, Willy rapidly screwed the tender handbrake hard down while Fred did the same for the engine. Both of them began to hurry towards the air raid shelter as the first of a stick of bombs came whistling down.

"Quick, Willy, no time to find the shelter! Here – back under our tender!" shouted Fred as he caught Willy by the collar and tugged him under the wheels. "We've got several tons of metal and coal over our heads, and the wheels may give us some sideways protection. Now lie flat!"

With that, Fred pushed Willy down, saying, "Mind your head on the pick-up scoop!"

Willy did as he was told but watched in horror as a bomb blew a small crater between two tracks forty yards away, just where they would have been had they continued running to the shelter. Two more bombs landed further away, one of them throwing a tank engine over on its side and smashing three ten-ton open trucks to matchwood. More bombs landed further away, destroying several vans and turning sidings into a tangled mass of twisted rails.

For the next twenty minutes, Fred and Willy cowered under their tender while more bombs fell on the dockyard sidings. There were occasional *pings* as bits of shrapnel hit the upper works of their engine, tender and wheels, and Willy heard Fred grunt as another bomb fell close to them, onto a wagon loaded with engineering parts. Finally the 'all clear' sounded and Willy crawled out from under the wheels.

He turned to his driver. "All clear now, Mr Leeming," he said, looking up to see a shunter with a First Aid bag and a hand lamp hurrying along the tracks.

The shunter stopped when he saw Willy.

"You OK, lad?" he asked.

Willy nodded as he climbed from under the tender, "We're fine, we hid under our tender here."

"What about your mate? Why doesn't he come out?"

"My driver?" Willy turned back and called, "All clear, Mr Leeming, you can come out now."

But Fred didn't move.

The shunter crouched down, "Let's have a look at him," he said, and lifted his lamp to get a better view then lowered it quickly so that Willy couldn't see.

"I think he's been hurt," he said to Willy, "Tell you what; you go to the shelter and get some blokes with a stretcher and I'll see what I can do here."

Willy hurried towards the shelter, making his way past several bomb craters. As he ran he heard the insistent clanging of an ambulance bell approaching. At the shelter, he was horrified to see three shapes lying on the ground covered by a tarpaulin; there were five more injured men sitting down being attended to by other railwaymen.

"You alright, young fellah?" asked one of the helpers, pausing to look up.

"We need a stretcher for my driver, we think he's injured," gasped Willy.

"Righto, where is he?"

"He's under the tender of the big 47; we'd just arrived from Acton when the bombing started so he said we should shelter under it."

"Man of sense," commented the helper as he gathered a First Aid bag and called two other men with a stretcher. The four of them made their way gingerly through the rubble to where the shunter was standing. He came over to Willy, while the stretcher bearers eased Fred from under the tender and lifted him on to the stretcher.

The shunter put his arm on Willy's shoulder and led him a few yards away. "Has he been your driver long?"

"About six months," said Willy, "Why?"

64

"Get on well with him, do you?"

"Yeah, he's one of the best drivers in our shed, and he's always showing me how to improve my firing. Is he OK?"

The shunter paused before answering. "I'm really sorry, lad."

Willy paled. "But he can't be badly hurt, we were under that bloody great tender. He was right next to me!"

"It looks like he was hit by a piece of strapping from a van or wagon."

"But..?" Willy couldn't believe what the shunter was telling him; then he saw the stretcher bearers carrying Fred to the shelter, a blanket covering his face and body. "They've covered his face! He's not..?"

"I'm afraid he is. The strapping punched through his chest; he wouldn't have known much about it."

Willy stopped and stared in shock at the men bearing the stretcher away. "But... but..?"

"We'd better get you to the First Aid post as well; we'll check you out before sending you home."

Two hours later, Willy was sitting on the fireman's seat in the cab of an old 43xx class 2-6-0 with two Chester enginemen. He had his right arm strapped up and his left elbow on the sill of the cab and he was staring out without seeing anything.

They were taking a short unfitted goods up to Ruabon and Aberystwyth; the Birkenhead foreman had decided to send Willy home with two of his colleagues. Driver Jack Shaw and his fireman Charlie Dalrymple, after a few words of condolence, tactfully left Willy to his misery. They had phoned through to Sid Thomson with the tragic news that he had lost one of his best and most experienced drivers.

The blow struck very hard among the one hundred and forty-odd enginemen employed at the shed, as Fred was acknowledged to be a great man to work with, especially to the younger cleaners and firemen, due to his wide experience and willingness to help others. Any fireman working with him had known that he would get driving experience as Fred would always insist on doing a couple of hours with the shovel - partly to keep himself fit, but mainly to give the fireman a chance to drive. He had claimed that his own drivers in the early 1900s had done the same for him and he was merely repaying a debt.

9 - Lance's bonus (August 1942)

Lance Hargreaves was sitting in a Liverpool pub, enjoying a pint, when he noticed an attractive young woman sitting at the next table. He had a couple of hours to kill until he was due back to fire for Jack Shaw on the Chester stopper from Birkenhead Woodside; Jack was not his regular driver, but George Denton was on a week's leave. Jack had suggested Lance go on the ferry to Liverpool, as he hadn't been there before.

The young woman had just finished her drink and stood to leave when Lance leaned over and asked if he could buy her another drink. She smiled and agreed, and came to sit next to him. 'My lucky day!', Lance thought to himself.

"You're a railwayman?" asked the girl, eying his shiny cap and blue overalls. Her name, she said, was Rosie.

"Yes, I've just finished part of a shift," answered Lance, "Then I'm off back home to Chester."

They chatted for half an hour and Lance decided to ask Rosie for her address and to perhaps meet her again; his firing trips to Birkenhead sometimes gave him enough time off that he would be able to pop across to Liverpool for a couple of hours.

"I usually have a drink in this pub here in Lime Street about this time," she said, "You'll almost certainly see me again!"

It was a gloomy, wet, autumn day with drizzle in the late afternoon as the semi-fast from Shrewsbury pulled in to Chester General on the far side into Platform Fourteen. Normally it would arrive in Number Three bay, but the Great Western sometimes had its longer trains directed into the LMS part of the station.

"You've done a good job today, young Lance!" said Jack to his fireman, "We'll make a driver of you yet!"

"Thank you, Mr Shaw," Lance replied, "But it wasn't so 'ard today, the engine was in good nick an' the coal warn't the rubbish they sometimes give us."

"Ah well, sometimes you get lucky. Now nip off and uncouple the coaches so we can move to the shed. We've made good time and we might be able to finish the shift a bit early, like."

Lance climbed down from the cab and released the steam and vacuum pipes. He was about to uncouple the engine when there was a shout of pain nearby. He looked up over the platform edge to see the driver of the Liverpool stopper on the next bay platform, helping his fireman down the cab steps.

Lance finished uncoupling his engine, climbed up and walked over to the other driver. "What's up? What 'appened?"

"My mate slipped on the greasy cab steps. I think he's done some damage to his leg." Lance could see blood running down through a tear in the fireman's right trouser leg.

"Yer'd better get 'im to some medical 'elp; that looks bad," said Lance, "Tell yer what, why don't you get on the phone fer a relief fireman and I'll take 'im to the LMS shed?"

"Would you do that? What about your own driver?"

"We've just finished our shift, 'e won't mind taking the engine to the shed and tellin' our foreman in the Western I'll be a bit late."

"You're a good fellah for a young 'un. What's your name?"

"Lance Hargreaves."

"Mine's Jeffrey McDonald. Our foreman's Jim Bailey and my fireman here is Derek Johnson."

"Righto, Mr McDonald, I'll see to 'im."

Lance hurried back over to his own driver to explain the situation.

Jack Shaw nodded, "Aye, I'll pass the word on to Sid." He lifted the regulator and eased the Hall class 4-6-0 forward to the points where it could reverse and back down to the GW shed for servicing.

In the meantime, Lance took the LMS fireman by the arm and started to walk him down the platform ramp and along the Crewe tracks towards the LMS shed, which was situated a quarter of a mile away.

The weather was still drizzling and the walk was difficult, as Derek's leg gave way several times and Lance had to hold him by the arm to stop him falling on the uneven cinder walkway. When they got to the shed, Derek, who had said very little, pointed to where the crewmen's First Aid centre was; they found a short, stout man with a bowler hat waiting for them.

"You'll be young Lance, I take it," said the man, "I'm Mr Bailey, and I'd like to thank you for your help today. We'll soon have Fireman Johnson sorted out, but I'd like you to come with me to my office."

The fireman was taken by another engineman to a small cabin for First Aid attention and Lance followed the foreman into his office.

"I've been on the phone to Sid in your shed and he tells me you might be young and only have three or four years' experience as a fireman, but you've got promise."

Lance was surprised to hear this; he had hitherto been used to receiving the sharp edge of the GW shed foreman's tongue. Praise was something he hadn't heard before.

Mr Bailey continued, "You could help us further. Jeff McDonald is now without a fireman on the Lime Street stopper and we haven't got a spare. I know you've just finished a shift and don't know the road to Lime Street, but could you help us out? Sid has agreed, if you'll be in it. It's not a long stint, only an hour or so, and you get paid extra for it, of course. You'd come back on the cushions."

Lance wasn't tired, even though he had just finished a shift. He knew Liverpool was a Luftwaffe target of course, but then so was Birkenhead which he knew well; there wasn't much difference. He thought also of the bonus and quickly agreed.

"Oh, I forgot," said Mr Bailey, "Have you ever fired an LMS engine?"

"Yes, once or twice. Last week in Salop we had to take over an LMS goods from Crewe to De Havilland at Codsall; we had an 8F on it."

"Good, you'll be right then, and many thanks. Now you'd better get back to the station, the Liverpool's due out in twenty minutes. It would be nice if it were on time in spite of the problem."

Back at the station, Jeff McDonald was pleased to see him. "The engine's ready, there's enough coal and we've 220 pounds pressure; we might need to top up the water somewhere though."

The engine was a 2-6-4 tank engine and so in spite of the continuing drizzle, they wouldn't get wet inside the roomy cab.

"Bit different from what you're used to, eh Lance?" commented Jeff.

"Not really, Mr McDonald," replied Lance, "Apart from me 'avin' to work on the right hand side of the cab, a lot of it seems similar to what we 'ave in our cabs."

"There's a reason for that; this engine is a Stanier design – he was trained as a Western man!"

Lance nodded approval whilst busily shovelling coal into the firebox, building up the fire. He didn't want to let the Great Western down and, more importantly, he wanted to confirm Mr Thomson's apparent faith in him.

In the meantime, the platform starter signal lifted and the driver had a quick look into the firebox, "That looks fine, now have a shufti outside and see if we've got the green."

As he spoke, the guard's whistle sounded and Lance saw the guard wave his green flag.

"Yeah, we've got it!" he replied.

The big tank engine with its eight coaches moved smoothly out of the station, past the long Number Three signal box, and curved left into the main LMS line to the north.

After passing the connection with the LNER line to Manchester at Mickle Trafford junction, the first stop was at Helsby, where a few passengers got in from the connecting Ellesmere Port train. Then they moved on to Frodsham. By this time, Lance was beginning to get the hang of the LMS tank engine; with frequent stops he was able to keep steam pressure at a satisfactory level and was enjoying the run in unfamiliar surroundings.

The approach to Lime Street station was made through streets which had already received plenty of attention from the German air force, but Lance was used to seeing shattered homes and streets. He had worked to Birkenhead on the other side of the River Mersey as well as to Wolverhampton and Birmingham.

The shed foreman at Edge Hill arranged for Lance to return on the next train to Chester, but pointed out that it wasn't due out for another ninety minutes. He could always cross the river on the ferry or the Mersey Railway and catch the train from Birkenhead, but Lance preferred to go back on the LMS route as he didn't know it.

"Well, thank you again, young man," said the Edge Hill shed foreman, "You've been a great help to us and I'll make sure to ring your boss and tell him so. In the meantime, you'll be getting a little something from the LMS in your next pay packet!"

"What's this I hear about my fireman going over to the LMS?" demanded George Denton, when Lance reported for duty two days later. Lance told him how he had helped out the LMS driver and Mr Denton nodded in approval.

"You'll do Lance, you'll do! You handled the Stanier tank engine well, says Jeff McDonald; I met him on the turntable yesterday. Now, today we're off again, first down to Woodside, and from there we go back up to Wrexham with a short goods and then light engine to Corwen to pick up the Birkenhead stopper back here."

As they were talking, Sid Thomson, the shed foreman, came over with an envelope in his hands. "Here you are young Lance, you lucky young devil, the LMS have expressed their appreciation of your efforts with a payment."

"How much did they pay him, Sid?" asked Mr Denton, "I would have given him an extra sixpence!"

"The LMS seem to think your fireman's worth more than that, George," Sid said, "They sent him five shillings!"

"Five bob? Just for an easy run to Liverpool? Money for jam," joked George, "I might transfer to the LMS, Sid!"

Lance said nothing but smiled as he happily slipped the coins into his pocket.

As they had a long wait in Birkenhead again, Lance decided to cross the Mersey on the ferry to Pierhead, catch a tram to Lime Street, and see if Rosie was in the pub he had met her in recently. He saw her straight away, sitting on her own. She smiled as she saw him and finished her drink.

"It's a bit noisy in here, let's go somewhere quieter," she said.

"Yeah, by all means!" replied Lance eagerly, "But, I don't know Liverpool at all."

"No difficulty about that – I've got a room not far away; would you like to see it?"

Would he! Lance couldn't believe his good fortune. They walked about ten minutes, and Rosie took out a key and unlocked the front door of a neat house in a row of terraced houses. She led the way up the stairs and into a small but comfortable room with an unusually large bed.

Once in the room, Rosie took her coat off then startled Lance by removing her blouse. His eyes nearly popped out of his head as she put her hands behind her back and unclipped her brassiere.

She stopped for a moment; "Have you got enough?"

"Enough?" Lance was puzzled.

Rosie leaned forward, smiling, and patted his bulging groin. "I don't mean enough of this, I mean money. It'll cost you five bob; I don't give it out for free!"

"Five bob?" Lance was shocked.

As she waited for his answer, Rosie hung her brassiere over a nearby drawer-knob; Lance, his mesmerized eyes glued to her bare breasts, slowly pulled two half-crowns out of his pocket and gave them to her silently.

On their way from Birkenhead with the Wrexham goods, George asked, "Had a good time in the Pool?"

Lance nodded thoughtfully.

"We've a bit of a wait in Corwen," said George, "So you can stand me a beer with some of that LMS bonus you got."

"Sorry Mr Denton," Lance suddenly found the gauge glass fascinating, "Er, it's all gone."

"You spent it all?" said George, startled.

"Yeah."

"What, five whole shillings?"

Lance nodded, examining the other gauges carefully.

George stared at him. "How the hell did you manage to spend..?" he paused, thought for a moment, then shouted with laughter. "You met one of the Lime Street tarts, you randy dog!"

But Lance didn't reply; he was now busy with his shovel.

10 - A difficult passenger (September 1942)

The 4-4-0 Midland Compound was running light engine and slowing down on the approach to Rhyl. Driver McDonald turned as his fireman looked to the left out of the cab behind him. They had run to Colwyn Bay and were returning to Rhyl to pick up a Chester stopper.

"What's the matter, mate?"

Derek Johnson said wistfully, "I wish we could chuck a few lumps of coal out here regularly; the company would never miss it!"

"What the hell for?" asked Jeff McDonald, startled.

"Look down there; you can just see the Marine Lake funfair."

"So?"

"Round the lake there's a fifteen-inch gauge miniature railway with a couple of engines in the little workshop. They haven't run since the war began because they can't get the coal."

"Oh, right."

"The missus and I come here every summer for our holiday," continued the fireman, "And young Malcolm - he's seven now - loves the Hall of Mirrors and the Coconut Shies; but he always stops in the little station and looks at the coaches. They've been parked there for three years. 'When will the train run again, Daddy?' he asks every year without fail."

"Yeah, I see what you mean; it's hard for the kids, especially if they knew what life was like before the War. Still, now the Yanks are with us, it shouldn't be long before it's all over. Keen on trains, is he?"

"I bought a Hornby Trains catalogue in 1940 when you could still get these things, and I think he pores over it every bloody day!"

"Think of the fun he'll have when they come back into the shops!"

As they coupled up to the seven non-corridors, Derek heard a loud *contralto* call from the platform: "I know there's a war on, you don't have to tell me that! But there's no excuse for sloppy standards. This train has no First Class carriages and I demand to know why!"

The speaker was an elderly lady dressed in a cardigan and a tweed skirt. She was complaining bitterly to Driver McDonald.

"I'm sorry Madam, I'm only the driver, I don't make up the train," answered Jeff McDonald, leaning on the side of his cab, "You should complain to the LMS management at Euston."

"That's not good enough! You railwaymen have had it easy while our brave boys are out there fighting for King and Country. All you do is to sit there in your nice warm cabs moving levers about and calling it work!"

Jeff McDonald was struck dumb at the sheer effrontery of the woman and was about to give her a piece of his mind when the guard's whistle went. He controlled himself with an effort and merely replied, "We're off now Madam, better get on the train if you're travelling."

With that he turned away and sounded the engine's whistle, taking hold of the regulator.

"You haven't heard the last of this!"

The angry woman stalked off to a compartment, fuming.

The driver lifted the regulator furiously. "Would you believe it! The cheek of the bloody woman! Who does she think she is?"

"I know who she is." Derek's quiet comment as he put a shovelful of coal into the firebox surprised his driver.

"What? You know her?"

"No, but I know of her. Steve duCane, a fireman from Crewe North, was talking about her once. Her name is Mrs Calthorpe and she lives in Rhyl apparently, and regularly travels to Chester. She always sits in the same seat in a compartment in the front coach so that she doesn't have far to go to beef to the driver. He says she always complains about something either when she gets on, or at

Chester when she gets off. They drive too fast, they stop too often, the seats are dirty or the train's late. She's a right complaining old biddy."

Jeff McDonald was silent for a moment. "Well she's complained once too often; I'll fix her."

"How?"

The driver smiled gently. "Wait and see, lad, wait and see. Now get busy, the scoop needs to go down, we're coming up to the troughs."

"Yes sir, certainly sir, three bags full, sir."

"Just get on with it, you cheeky young sod."

During the rest of the run to Chester, Jeff McDonald was unusually silent, but he had a glint in his eye that made his fireman feel rather sorry for Mrs Calthorpe. Driver McDonald, as Derek well knew, was not one to make empty threats.

After he had climbed back into the cab from uncoupling the engine at Chester's Number Nine platform, Derek noticed his driver signal to the crew of a down train waiting on Platform Four. Curious, he watched as his driver dropped from the cab and walked across the tracks to chat to the fireman, who had descended from the cab of the Black Five. The fireman was Steve duCane.

A few moments later, Derek's driver climbed back into the cab and said, "Righto Derek my lad, time you did a bit of driving. Let's have that shovel and I'll pull some of the coal forward while you can take us to the shed for servicing."

"Wasn't that Steve duCane on the down Llandudno you were talking to?"

"I think that's his name. Why, what's that to you?" Jeff's answer was curt.

"Oh, er, nothing." Derek knew when it was wise to break off the conversation. He concentrated on watching for the platform starter to clear for them to move forward along the Crewe line to the LMS shed, past Chester Number Three signal box and under the road bridge. Their engine needed to be turned and prepared for the next crew.

Going off duty, Derek noticed that instead of walking to the bike shed, his driver went to Jim Bailey's office, apparently to talk to the shed foreman.

The Midland Compound 4-4-0, scheduled for the week on the North Wales run with Driver McDonald and Fireman Johnson, was in surprisingly good condition, having just come from repair at Derby Works. The pair enjoyed their shifts on it.

However, on the Thursday, Jeff said, "I'm getting a bit fat, I need some exercise on the shovel. When we leave Rhyl you're driving as far as Mostyn, so I can get some firing done."

Derek was delighted; like all firemen, he enjoyed the chance to get in some driving practice and he agreed instantly. He felt elated as he eased the train away from the platform in Rhyl onto the up slow line, but wondered what was so interesting to his driver who had been watching the passengers board the train.

As the train gathered speed, Driver McDonald busied himself with the shovel and a few minutes later stuck his head out of the cab to watch for the water troughs. Derek watched him drop down the scoop to pick up the water, but he wound it back rather late, and water squirted out of the overflow pipes and over the tender and first coach of the train.

'Bit out of practice!' thought Derek, but he wasn't foolish enough to say it out loud.

In the first coach of the same train, Steve duCane and his driver were relaxing 'on the cushions', returning from their shift. Steve was sitting with his back to the engine, opposite the lady who was so fond of complaining. She was sitting at the window seat, reading a book.

Steve took out a cigarette and asked Mrs Calthorpe very politely if she would object to him smoking. She said, "It's a disgusting habit, young man, and I shall want the window wide open while you do."

Taking this as agreement, Steve opened the window, lit

his cigarette, and puffed away contentedly for a couple of minutes. Then he stood up and closed the window, saying, "I think it would be wise to close the window for a short time."

The lady stood up and hauled the window right down again.

"Nonsense!" she said, "As long you have that horrible thing in your mouth, I need fresh air!"

Steve shrugged his shoulders. "If you insist!"

The lady sat down again and picked up her book, continuing to read until there was a sudden *Whoosh!* as a huge shower of cold water sprayed through the window, soaking her to the skin and turning her book into a sodden mess.

"Oh dear!" exclaimed Steve, and he offered her a handkerchief. Steve's driver, Harry Percival, sitting next to him, coughed, and his shoulders shook as he tried hard to control his laughter.

The lady herself was speechless and furiously angry. "You knew that was going to happen! My book is ruined and you'll have to pay for it!" she shouted at Steve, "I will make a formal complaint to LMS management!"

"I'm afraid that won't help you, Madam," Harry chimed in, "You and I both clearly heard my fireman offer to close the window for a few moments, and I will say so if Mr duCane is called to account."

As the train drew up at Prestatyn, Harry and his fireman stood up and left the compartment. Mrs Calthorpe also left the compartment, slamming the door, and stamped over to the Ladies toilet, wringing out her cardigan to clean up and dry herself. Harry and Steve walked along the platform to the cab and climbed in to join Jeff and Derek.

"Worked a treat!" laughed Steve to the driver, "Your slowness with the pick-up scoop did the trick nicely. The spray from the overfilled tank gave her an unexpected bath! She had to leave the train and go to the Ladies' bog and tart herself up, and the next up train is a semi-fast and doesn't stop here!"

"Well she might not be so keen to insult railwaymen in future!" chuckled Jeff. "When I spoke to Jim Bailey about getting you two on the cushions from Rhyl, he agreed instantly – he's had a few complaints about her himself."

On arriving at Chester there was a thick fog. On Platform Nine, an inspector was waiting. "You'll have to take the train on to Crewe as Empty Coaching Stock," he said to Jeff, "They're needed for a train to Stoke. You can come back from Crewe on the cushions. This means a bit of overtime."

"Righto, but when do we leave?"

"There's a goods for Stafford just ahead of you; I'll get it backed into a refuge at Beeston and then you can go through."

"Good; we've time for a quick brew then."

Jeff and his fireman sat and relaxed for ten minutes with their tea, until the starter signal clanged up and it was time to depart.

The fog at Beeston was equally heavy and Driver Jack Strawson in his LMS 8F heavy freight engine was backing his train slowly into the refuge siding to clear the line for the passenger ECS through to Crewe. However, the oil lamp on the front of the engine, unknown to both him and Fireman Simon Hinks, had gone out. Simon had forgotten to check the oil level when preparing the engine.

"Can't stand bloody fog!" grumbled Jack, staring out of the cab, "Keep a sharp eye open for the signal."

"I might 'ave to climb out and walk to it, mate," said Simon, "I can't see owt."

As the signalman could not see the engine lamp, nor even the engine itself, he was not sure whether it was fully in the refuge. He had had a long shift in cold and miserable weather and should have gone out of his warm signal box to check the position of the goods; but he had a cold already and did not want to make it worse, and so pulled an old and very dangerous ploy. He unlocked the signal lever and tried to slide it over, reasoning that if the

79

train was still over the points, the lever would not move. The lever slid over easily and so the signalman set the points for the passenger train to go through, believing that the goods train was now safely in the refuge and assuming the driver was clear of the fouling point. He then signalled to allow the ECS through.

However, although much of the goods was in the refuge, the engine and a dozen wagons were still on the main line, just backing past the signal as it changed. The point-blade had moved easily because just as the bobby pulled the lever, a long wheelbase wagon had been traversing it and the blades had moved without hindrance.

"Hey up! There we go!" said Simon as he heard the clang and glimpsed the signal change, "P'raps the bobby 'eard that the ECS was late, an' 'e's lettin' us go forward to Calveley."

"Right," answered Jack and he stopped the train and reversed its direction. With the wagons' wheel flanges squealing on the wet track, the goods train began to move forward again. But the point change had the effect of derailing all the goods vehicles still in the refuge as they were drawn out again.

"What's that noise?" wondered Simon, hearing the rattling sound behind them.

Jack listened for a moment and then swore. "We're off the bloody road!" he shouted, "That's our wagons derailing!"

He shut off steam quickly and the engine came to a stand.

"Get out quick, Simon, and run and inform the bobby, we're blocking the main line. God, there'll be hell to pay!"

But hell arrived faster even than they expected. Just as Simon reached the signal box, the Empty Coaching Stock train from Chester ran into the derailed goods train. Fortunately, Jeff McDonald had been driving fairly slowly due to the fog, and although the engine smashed two open wagons as it hit them and derailed, it did not tip over.

Jeff and Derek were both badly shaken as the engine jerked to a stop, with steam bursting out of the right hand cylinder and two planks from a wagon rearing up and landing on the tender. Driver Jack Strawson of the 8F was too far ahead to suffer any injury, but he heard the crash and hurried back to see what he could do to help. The freight guard was extremely lucky. Hearing the derailments, he had climbed down from his van and seen the approaching passenger train in time to jump aside as it hit the goods train.

The breakdown crane gang from Crewe took several hours to clear up the mess, and although Simon Hinks received a severe reprimand for forgetting to check the oil lamp, the signalman was not so lucky; he was demoted to Porter at Crewe. Because the passenger train was an ECS train, there were no other people hurt, apart from the passenger guard who spilt hot tea over himself.

Jim Bailey, the foreman at Chester LMS shed, had the last word when Driver McDonald and Fireman Johnson reported off duty later that night.

"I'm very disappointed in you two," he said shaking his head sadly, "I give you a very nice engine in good nick straight from the repair shop to play with, and what d'you do for me? Only a week later you bring it back to me all bent!"

11 - Lance develops a new skill (December 1942)

George Denton came into the crew cabin one morning looking for his fireman.

Finding him relaxing with his feet up on the little coal heater, he said, "Now then, Lance my lad, we're going to extend your abilities. You're going to learn the road south from Brum. As from tomorrow we're scheduled on the 11.45 from Birkenhead. We break at Wolverhampton as usual, but instead of coming back on the 4.10 Paddington, we join the Old Oak Common crew and go on with them so you can learn the road to Paddington!"

Lance was pleased. "That's good news for me Mr D., but what about staying the night in London? Couldn't that be a bit dicey?"

"Dicey? Why? The crewmen's digs won't be the Ritz, but they'll be OK."

"No, I was thinkin' of the bombin'."

"Oh, that! No, it won't be anything special just for us – just the usual that Londoners put up with."

"Oh yeah, of course."

"Worried about the bombing, are you?"

Lance shrugged in some embarrassment.

"A bit," he admitted.

"Well stop worrying; if it's got your name on it, there's nothing you can do about it. Worrying won't improve your chances and might distract you from your job."

"Yeah, sorry."

George added, "There's a bonus, of course, you haven't realized yet."

"Oh, what's that?"

"We change engines at Wolverhampton."

"C'mon Mr D. I'm not stupid. I know that, it means..?" His face lit up, "The 11.45 is a heavy train!"

"Right!"

"It might be a King!"

"Not quite."

Lance's face fell, "Not a King?"

"No; not 'it *might* be a King'. It *will* be a King."

The heavy King class 4-6-0s were the pride of the Great Western Railway fleet; they could handle the heaviest of trains at express speeds. However, although the crews generally enjoyed working on them, with their twelve-foot-deep fireboxes they kept the firemen very busy. Northern crews very rarely got their hands on them as Kings were not permitted north of Wolverhampton because of their weight and the fact that their cylinders were too wide for some of the platforms. The generous loading gauge south of Wolverhampton was designed in the days of the old broad gauge which had never reached any further north.

"But hold your horses, you won't be firing while you're learning the road. You'll be observing."

"Do you know the road to Paddington?"

"Yes, I was based at Salop for a while and we had occasional double home turns to Paddington if there were crew shortages at Stafford Road."

"Well if I won't be firing, what's the point of me learnin' the road?"

George sighed. "For a bright lad, you can be remarkably daft at times. I said you won't be firing while you're learning the road. You will be later, and in any case, the wider your knowledge of the roads is, the better your chances of promotion."

"Oh yeah, didn't think of that."

"Well now think of visiting the stores for oil and cotton waste, we've got an engine to prepare."

The weather was cold and it had begun to snow during the night. Lance and George were happy when they could get back into the cab of their Castle class express passenger engine. George had been shivering as he had gone round to oil the motion and was glad to warm his hands when the firebox doors were open.

As they were taking their train under the corner of Chester's City's Walls, there were two thumping sounds on the backhead and two blobs of snow began trickling down.

"What was that?" Lance had been turning to pick up another shovelful of coal for the firebox. He looked up to his driver in puzzlement.

"Nothing to worry about, just a couple of school kids chucking snowballs into the cab as we go past. They hide in the bushes just here or the stand on the bridge and try and drop snowballs down the chimney! Little devils!"

Lance straightened up, glaring at the bushes which were now drifting far away as the train accelerated towards the signal gantry before the Dee Bridge. He caught a quick glimpse of two small figures in school uniforms among the bushes they had just passed.

"Just you wait, yer little buggers, I'll 'ave yer fer that!" he muttered to himself.

At Wolverhampton there was a surprise. George and Lance had uncoupled their Castle and a Stafford Road crew had taken it to the shed so that they could stay and climb into the cab of the waiting King. Driver Allan Stevenson and his fireman Alf Murgatroyd greeted them aboard with the welcome news that a derailment ahead meant that they had a fifteen minute delay, enough time for a spot of breakfast. The Old Oak Common crew had even brought some extra bacon and a couple of eggs; this was an unusual treat as, after three years of war, most food was strictly rationed and the rations were anything but generous.

"OK, young Lance," said Driver Stevenson after they had introduced themselves, "You can start work by cleaning Alf's shovel; there's a bit of cotton waste for you in the corner."

The cotton waste and a good squirt from the coal watering pipe ensured that the shovel was clean enough, so the bacon and eggs were dropped onto it. Alf opened the fire-doors and eased the shovel over the flames in the great firebox; a few moments later the glorious smell of frying bacon spread through the cab.

With bellies full of fried bread, bacon, eggs and tea, the four men were very much at ease when the starter signal dropped. Allan lifted the regulator to move the express off on its journey towards Paddington. The next stop was Birmingham Snow Hill.

While waiting at the platform at Snow Hill, Alf picked up two smallish pieces of coal, tapped a couple of corners off them with his coal pick so that they were somewhat rounder, and showed them to his driver.

Allan looked carefully at Alf's left hand and said, "Try that one."

George began to grin as Allan turned to him. "What d'you think, George?"

"I'd clean forgotten about that!" he said, laughing. He studied them and then also pointed to the left-hand lump, "Yep, that one should do it."

Lance was totally mystified. "What the 'ell are you lot on about?"

"Wait and see!" said George, as Alf placed the selected lump of coal carefully on the shelf in front of the toolbox.

The whistle went and the guard's green flag waved from the rear of the train. 'We've got the green," said Alf to Allan. Allan lifted the regulator and the huge King began to move effortlessly with its sixteen coaches, away from the platform and into the long tunnel.

Alf put a few more shovelfuls around the firebox, and then handed the shovel to Lance, "'Ere yer go, mate, put a 'alf a dozen down the front!"

Lance, delighted at the thought of firing a King, grabbed the shovel and swung it round to the tender, filled it and threw the first load into the firebox.

"Can't hear the bell!" said Allan, listening with a hand cupped to his ear. "You'll have to throw it further!"

"Bell? What bell?" asked Lance as he paused, surprised.

"Oh, didn't you know? You have to throw the first shovelful almost twelve feet down the firebox of a King to ring the bell!"

Lance thought for a moment, lowered the shovel and pushed his left leg towards Allan. "There yer go!" he said to him, "Now pull the other one!"

Allan cackled and said to George, "Crikey, George, you've got a cheeky young bugger there!"

In the meantime, Alf was standing on the tender footplate, weighing the lump of coal ready in his hand and staring ahead.

"Nearly there!" he said.

As they swept out of the tunnel past the smaller Moor Street terminus on their right, they began to see a number of gardens backing on to the railway. Alf moved to give his arm room for a good swing and then hurled the lump of coal into one of the gardens. Lance saw it just miss a chamber pot set up on a post and land in a net spread behind the pot. There were half a dozen lumps of coal on the ground near the net, showing where other engine crews had tried their luck.

George chuckled and nudged Lance. "The owner of that garden never has to buy any coal for his fire – he gets it all from the Great Western Railway for free! He only needs to buy a potty occasionally!"

Lance nodded, saying, "I think I'll 'ave a go on the way back; I used ter be good at chuckin' rocks."

"Well never mind about chucking rocks now, just keep your eyes peeled for signals and such; you're supposed to be learning the road."

There were no further delays, but the approach to Paddington was slow. Although the signals were easy to see in the blackout without street lights to confuse things, there was heavy rail traffic and delays were frequent. The cab was also very stuffy because, to prevent the light of the fire being easily visible to enemy bombers overhead, the glass side windows had been plated over and the gap between the cab roof and tender was closed in by a tarpaulin. Alf showed Lance where the signals were to be found and there were many of them, especially when they joined the main line from the west; the signal gantries showed a confusing array.

"Don't worry, Lance,' said Alf, "You'll get used to them soon and know which ones to look for."

The landlady at their London accommodation was the elderly widow of a railwayman and, although the place was clean, she was parsimonious with food and begrudged the men a second cup of tea.

"Evil-tempered old bat!" commented George to Lance next day on their way back to the shed, until he heard from the Old Oak Common men that her husband had been killed in the bombing and her son was a merchant seaman away at sea.

"Ah, well, I suppose she's got grounds for complaint about life," he said later, "Let's be charitable."

At their next visit, George gave her a small packet of tea saved from his ration. She smiled briefly as she thanked him and the atmosphere in the digs mellowed slightly for the next few days.

The days went past without undue incident and Lance was surprised that, after five trips, he knew where to watch out for most of the signals, and was even able to help Alf on the run in to Paddington, allowing the latter to concentrate on his firing.

On their last run on the 11.10 from Paddington, when they climbed into the cab, Alf gave Lance his shovel and said, "She's all yours now Lance, me lad. Let's see whether you can fire a King! You can 'ave her as far as Brum, and I'll do the last stretch to Wolverhampton."

"You're sure?"

"Yeah, don't worry; me driver's agreed and I'll watch what you're doin' and see yer don't do anythin' daft!"

"Ta very much!" Lance was pleased and proud that he'd been entrusted to fire a King; "But listen," he added, "would yer mind if we changed over a bit earlier, say, near Warwick; I want to 'ave a go at that pot!"

Both driver and fireman laughed and Allan clapped him on the shoulder, "You'll do, mate, you'll do!"

George, watching all this, pulled a coin out of his

pocket and said quietly to Allan, "Half a crown says he'll hit the pot!"

He placed the coin on the firebox shelf.

Allan smiled and answered, "I'm happy to take your money, George; it's harder than it looks. Alf here's a good shot and he hasn't hit it yet."

With that, another half-crown joined George's on the shelf.

Lance was very tired and relieved when, shortly after leaving Leamington Spa, Alf took the shovel from him and said, "I'll 'ave 'er now Lance; yer did well! Now find yerself a decent lump o' coal!"

With the coal hammer, Lance rounded a corner off a smallish lump and put it ready near the tender toolbox.

"You've got about three minutes, Lance!" said Allan, looking out of the cab window, "Then I can put five bob in my pocket!"

"Don't count your chickens, Allan," warned George with a grin, "I told you, he's a dead shot!"

"Comin' up!" called Alf, watching out of the cab. Lance took the lump in his right hand and let fly. The piece of coal shot down the garden and shattered the potty into a thousand pieces before joining the many other lumps of coal under the net.

"Cor!" Alf was staggered, "Yer jammy devil!"

"Bloody good shot!" said Allan and gestured to George to pick up the coins on the firebox shelf.

George reached over to the two half crowns, put one in his pocket and handed the other to Lance, remarking, "Save that for your next visit to Lime Street!"

"Lime Street?" said Allan in surprise, "That's LMS. Do you two go to Liverpool?"

"No, we only go to Woodside, but Lance nips across the Mersey once in a while; he's got a friend over there."

George winked at Lance whose face, previously rather smug at his throwing accuracy, became red as he turned quickly, pretending to look out of the cab for a signal.

At Wolverhampton the two crews shook hands; they had become friends after the co-operation, and promised to look out for each other when next they met at Stafford Road.

Next week, although George and Lance no longer continued on to Paddington, they still had the 11.45 out of Birkenhead to take to Wolverhampton, which meant that they passed the City Walls at school lunch time.

As it was snowing again, Lance said to George as they went through the long tunnel, "I'm goin' to 'ave a go at them school kids if they're there."

He made a couple of snowballs from off the tender and placed them ready. Sure enough, they glimpsed two school caps among the bushes as they hurried past, and Lance fired off one of the snowballs. They saw the snowball hit one of the boys full in the face as he was preparing to throw his own into the cab; the second lad was so surprised that he dropped the snowball he was about to throw.

"Yer can 'ave the second snowball termorrer, yer little sods!" called out Lance as they accelerated towards the signal gantry in the distance.

"That's a handy skill you've developed there, Lance," chuckled George, "If you ever get the Paddington run, that bloke near Snow Hill will have to buy himself a whole row of potties!"

Then he paused and asked, "By the way, can your mum cook rabbit pie?"

"Yeah, she also makes a nice rabbit stew; why? Yer can't get rabbits fer love nor money."

"I've just realized; in the summer, we might get the Corwen run again, and just past Llangollen there's a rabbit colony. If we get stopped at a signal you might be able to knock off a couple of coneys. My missus cooks them well too."

"I'll remember to keep me 'and in with the throwin'," answered Lance as he bent down with the shovel.

12 - All in a day's work (April 1943)

It was a cool but sunny day in early April as Driver Len Snaith of Wellington shed eased his train into the bay at the south end of Crewe station. He stopped a few yards from the buffers, shut off the regulator and screwed down the brake. He then removed the notebook from the little pocket in the roof of his cab and noted the time of arrival.

While he was doing this, his fireman, Geoff Hodgson, jumped down onto the platform and down again onto the track to uncouple the coaches. Climbing back onto the footplate, he began to reposition the oil lamps. All this was observed with amusement by the driver of the large, streamlined LMS Duchess class express locomotive. In her wartime black paint and looking like a long black bullet, the train was waiting on the main through road for a London express due in nine minutes. The engine of the Liverpool would come off in Crewe and Driver Harold Edwards would couple his Duchess on and take the express the rest of the way to Euston, stopping only at Stafford and Rugby.

"Hey Alf, come and look at this!" he called to his fireman.

Alf came over with a cup of tea in his hand, "What's up?"

"Have a gander at what's come into the bay here; I always knew the Great Western was old fashioned, but this is ridiculous!"

They stared, amused, at the Great Western engine; it was a little 4-4-0 with a long funnel, a huge steam dome and outside frames.

Harold cackled, leaned out of his cab and called over to Len, "Hey mate, what's that you're driving?"

"This?" called Len, leaning out of his cab and patting the side, "This is the perfect little branch line engine,

90

only seven years old!"

"What?" Harold calculated in his mind for a moment, "1936? Never!"

"Straight up, 1936 it was; cannibalised in Swindon from two other engines, and nice little runners they are too."

"1936 bollocks, mate; they're having you on. It was *1836*!"

"Alright, it does look a bit old fashioned, but at least it looks like a proper engine, not like yours. By the way, are you a Crewe North man?"

Harold frowned and said "No, we're Edge Hill, why?"

"Ah, that explains it; Lancastrians – I suppose that's why you're driving that long black pudding."

Harold's fireman laughed in delight. "He's got you there mate, you shouldn't have insulted his little engine!"

Harold called over to Len, "Yes, well this long black pudding can take sixteen on at eighty miles an hour; your little antique can't do that!"

"No, you're quite right," came the prompt reply, "But this little antique can get its six coaches into the bay at Wellington *and* fit on the 35 foot turntable there. Your black pudding can't do that!"

"You'll have to give up, Harold, he's too quick for you. Anyway," Alf said, looking north up the platform, here's the Liverpool coming in, and it's got... what the hell's that bringing it in? It's got the number plate of a Scot on the front, but I've never seen a Scot looking like that; its boiler's been tapered!"

There was a call from the bay as the Great Western engine slowly backed out.

"That's one of your LMS Scots coming in," shouted Len, pointing from the cab with a grin, "It's been rebuilt by Stanier to look like a Great Western loco – it looks more like a proper engine now!"

With that, the Great Western engine scuttled southwards out of the station.

Alf began to check the steam pressure and shovel coal into the firebox as Harold eased the great Duchess forward to the points in order to back onto the Euston express.

"GWR three, LMS nil," muttered Alf, chuckling to himself.

In the meantime, the Great Western crew turned on the triangle at Crewe South and made their way to the small shed at Gresty Lane which the Great Western maintained (as a sub-shed of Wellington) in the very heart of LMS territory. It always amused Len that the GWR often shedded its oldest engines there, as if to suggest that Crewe didn't deserve anything better.

But in fact the little 4-4-0s had been a highly successful conversion in which older Duke class boilers had been placed on scrapped Bulldog class frames to produce very handy little general purpose engines. When first built, they had been given the names of earls of the realm, but when the earls saw them they were highly indignant, demanding that their names be given to larger and more impressive locomotives, and so the names were removed and replaced on modern Castle class express engines. The little engines were then nicknamed 'Dukedogs' and used for a variety of purposes on lighter routes.

After servicing at Gresty Lane shed, Len and Geoff returned to Crewe station to back onto the Wellington local once more. Arriving at Wellington they were then scheduled to take a short parcels train to Chester via Shrewsbury and Wrexham.

When they stopped at Platform Four at Shrewsbury, the driver of an LMS Patriot class engine, waiting on the centre track to pick up a Bristol to York through train, leaned out from his cab and called across to them.

"Just come in from the nineteenth century, have you?"

"What's with these LMS drivers?" grumbled Geoff to his driver, then he leaned out and gave the LMS crew a Churchillian gesture but with the hand reversed.

"They don't recognize quality when they see it," answered Len loudly, looking across at them, "They're just jealous. Don't worry about it."

Two hours later, in Chester shed for servicing, they watched as an LMS 0-6-0 Jinty trundled past to stop and reverse to pick up a couple of coaches from the carriage sidings on the Birkenhead triangle. It slowly drew up to the station throat signals where Len and Geoff were also waiting. The driver leaned out with a friendly wave, and Len waved back, calling out, "Did you know your left inside cylinder head seems to be leaking?"

"Damn thing's always leaking," replied the Jinty driver, "This is the Chester station pilot and we all call it 'Piddling Peter'!"

"Sounds like the right name for it!" laughed Len, "Is it any good?"

"Yeah, apart from the leaking, she's a good little runner." The driver studied the Dukedog carefully. "Haven't seen one like yours before, I bet she can perform too, when she has to."

"Dead right, mate." Len turned to his fireman, "There you go, Geoff, not all LMS men are twerps!"

They backed onto the half-dozen coaches in Platform Two bay with a stopper for Shrewsbury, coupled up, and waited for the starter to drop.

While they were waiting, Len commented to Geoff, "It's been a long shift today, a bit of mileage over the limit, so a few more bob in the pocket. Now for a quiet run to Salop and then light engine home."

However, in this optimistic opinion Len was gravely in error.

"Look at the way those blokes are earning the King's shilling!" exclaimed Geoff in disgust as they stood in Ruabon station. There were five soldiers on the opposite platform kicking a rubbish bin around, "One of 'em's even a corporal!"

Just then, an ancient porter came out of the waiting room and gave the soldiers a piece of his mind, but they ignored him and kicked the bin onto the track. One of them climbed down to pick it up.

"I'm tempted to give them a squirt with the coal watering pipe," growled Geoff, but Len just looked at him.

"Only a thought!" said Geoff.

93

A short while later, as they were travelling at some speed, they heard a loud *rat-at-tat!* and the roar of an aircraft engine. They looked up to see a Focke-Wolf scream low overhead.

"Good God!" shouted Geoff, "At least the bugger missed us!"

"The sod's coming round again!" said Len, watching the aircraft begin a long, easy turn. "He's missed the first time and he's coming round again; he's going to try and drill the boiler!"

"What'll we do, can we go faster?"

"If we speed up just as he comes again he's likely to miss us and put the shells into the carriages. We can't let him do that. Just watch him carefully and get ready to slam the emergency brake on. But wait till I tell you!"

They waited as the aircraft closed and lined itself up to attack again. Len waited, watching the aircraft carefully, and when it was only about three hundred yards away he shouted, "Now!"

The train immediately slowed down and came to a stand as the bullets peppered past the front of the engine. The aircraft began a slow second turn.

Len said, "Quick Geoff, we'll get along the train and get everyone out and flat on the ground!"

They jumped down as heads popped out of the windows to see what the sudden stop was about.

"Everyone out! We are being attacked by a Jerry fighter! Out and flat on the ground!"

People began to scramble out of the train and scatter into the fields, but from the third coach a dozen soldiers jumped out. They settled in a disciplined row under a coach with their rifles and prepared to fire back. As the aircraft came again, they began to fire at long range. The pilot jerked away from his long attacking glide and soared away without opening fire.

The guard and Geoff began to collect the passengers and chivvy them back on the train.

Len sought out the group of soldiers who were still standing next to the train and said, "I reckon you lot saved our bacon today. We are all very grateful indeed to you. It's only a pity you couldn't have knocked him out of the sky."

Their sergeant, an older man, answered, "It's very hard to hit a speeding aircraft with the standard Army 303 rifle; we had plenty of practice at Dunkirk a couple of years back. You were lucky we were on the train with ammunition; we'd just come back from an exercise using live rounds. Normally we wouldn't be travelling with live ammo."

"Well anyway, many thanks mate; you've saved a few lives, not to mention a train. I bet that German pilot was surprised to find himself shot at!"

"All part of the service, but we can't be sure he's gone yet," muttered the sergeant, staring around and called to his corporal, "Jack, get the Bren out, you never know."

"We didn't have time for the machine gun before," he explained to Len.

The corporal opened a long box and took out a light machine gun. He put it on the ground, opening the two front supports, and snapped a curved magazine of twenty-nine rounds onto the gun, placing three or four more magazines on the ground next to it.

Suddenly the sergeant shouted, "Down lads! Here he comes again!"

He was looking back along the train and saw the aircraft some distance away and approaching from behind. "Get ready, Jack!"

The corporal dropped down flat behind the Bren and took aim at the still distant fighter. The other soldiers were also lying down with their rifles aimed.

The machine gun opened up, and Len and Geoff on the ground were astonished to be able to see the bullets going off like a string of fire. The first magazine was emptied and ripped off. A second one was snapped on rapidly and the Bren opened up again. By this time the pilot had curved away again, followed by the stream of bullets from the Bren and now by rifle fire. As he turned, they could see a few holes in his left wing, but otherwise no damage was apparent.

"That's it, I think," said the sergeant, "He now knows we're not helpless. He won't be back this time, he's not stupid."

"Very impressive!" said Len.

"Yeah, the tracer's a great help," commented the sergeant, "Otherwise he might not have known he was being fired on; a few tracer rounds in the clip makes a fine sight."

They got the passengers back on board and moved off again, only to stop at the next signal box to report what had happened and to explain why they were running late.

Arriving in Shrewsbury, Geoff uncoupled the coaches while Len went to report the events in greater detail. They then drove light engine back to Wellington to book off.

"Heard you had a bit of excitement," commented the foreman as they entered the office.

"Smart-arse LMS drivers, bloody-minded German fighter pilots and a handy Army unit," shrugged Len. "All in a day's work!"

13 - A matter of faith (October 1943)

The two men were sitting in the warmth of the enginemen's cabin and enjoying a quick brew before checking out the board on which the details of their day's duty lay. It was a cold day and Driver Ron Smithers and his fireman Danny Cohen of Crewe North shed were discussing the possibilities of their new schedule.

"Up you get, Danny. Go and see what we've got on the Holyhead this morning," Ron said to his fireman, "While I finish my tea."

A few moments later, Danny came back. "They've given us a Scot, number 6135, do you know her?"

Ron frowned, "6135? She's not one of ours, I hope she's not been dumped on us from somewhere that doesn't want her."

His neighbour, Driver Jack Hamilton, leaned over and said, "Don't worry Ron, she's not bad at all. We 'ad 'er a couple o' days back on a running in turn to Salop an' back. She's just out o' the works."

"Oh right Jack, that's good to hear, did she pull well?"

"Don't really know – she seemed fine but we only 'ad seven bogies there an' back."

"Mmmm... the Holyhead'll have twice that, it's a heavy train. Why was she in the works?"

"She's bin rebuilt – looks like a Great Western engine now!"

"Oh, one of the rebuilt Scots? I've never had one of them."

The big Royal Scot class 4-6-0s had been a godsend to the LMS when they were built in 1927; the newly formed LMS had been in dire straits with its express passenger traffic. The mainstay of the West Coast expresses had been the ex-LNWR Claughtons which were well past their best, and were disliked by the ex-Midland men because they were heavy on coal (and, it must be admitted,

97

because they weren't Midland designs).

However, the Midland was only able to offer their small 4-4-0 Compounds, which required double-heading with the heavier trains. The Great Western had been asked for drawings of their highly successful Castles, but they had refused the request. When the Scots arrived, they proved easily capable of handling the heavy West Coast passenger traffic. Now, after sixteen years including four years of war, they were getting rough. They were gradually being rebuilt by William Stanier, the Chief Mechanical Engineer, who hailed from the Great Western Railway and had totally rejuvenated the LMS locomotive fleet with his range of versatile engines.

Ron and Danny collected their engine and got the feel of it as they took it to the spur next to the main down platform and waited for the Holyhead express from Euston to arrive. This was on time and hauled by a big, grimy, streamlined Crewe North Pacific which uncoupled and moved on to the shed for servicing. Ron backed the Scot onto the train as Danny climbed down to couple up and connect the steam heating gear and vacuum pipes.

As they pulled away towards Chester round to the left past the great works on their right, Ron said to Danny, "We'll soon see if she's any good, the guard tells me she's got fourteen bogies on her tail."

"Good job there's no steep gradients between here and Holyhead, then," commented Danny, "But with fourteen on, I may have a bit of shovelling to do!"

By the time they had reached Rhyl on the coast, they realized that they had an engine in top notch condition and were enjoying the experience. It was very rare for a crew to get what was effectively a brand new engine straight from Crewe Works.

"I saw a long troop train coming from Liverpool the other day," remarked Ron, "Full of Yanks it was; I heard there's talk of opening a second front in France now that we're in Italy."

"Probably off one of the big troopships. Nice to have

them, but what do they know about fighting? We've been at it for five years."

"Don't forget, some of the Yanks have been in North Africa and Italy already; they'll know the odds."

"Yeah, but the ones from the troopships will be fresh and untried."

"They'll soon learn - and in any case many of our troops are new recruits too. Anyway, forget the squaddies for now," Ron changed the subject, "Let's enjoy running an engine in top nick; we've only got stops at Llandudno Junction and Bangor before we get to Holyhead. Get your back ready, I'm going to open her up now that we've left Rhyl!"

And open her up he did. They raced through Abergele and Colwyn Bay as the Scot performed effortlessly. Upon approaching the Britannia tubular bridge after leaving Bangor, Danny shut the firebox doors. The bridge had a very low roof and a sudden change of air pressure between the cab and the firebox could cause a blow-back. A blow-back was an engineman's nightmare as the cab could be filled with fire.

Shortly after crossing the Menai Strait they passed through the little station famous all over the world for its 57-letter nameboard along the length of the platform, but known to the locals as Llanfair P. G. They arrived in Holyhead ten minutes ahead of schedule and would have done even better, if Ron hadn't decided to play safe and slow down; arriving well before their booked time could cause locomotive inspectors to ask awkward questions.

Holyhead shed supplied much-needed tea, and they had a two-hour break before they returned to Crewe. An hour before they were due to leave again, they were approached by a young Passed Cleaner who requested a lift in the cab as far as Rhyl in return for doing a bit of help.

Danny looked at Ron, "I've no objection to getting some of my heavy work done by someone else," he laughed.

Ron looked deep in thought at the young man and finally

agreed, "Yeah, OK."

"Thanks mates," said the young man, "My name's Arthur, Arthur McKinlay. Rhyl's my home shed."

Danny shook Arthur's hand and said, "Welcome aboard; I'm Danny, Danny Cohen."

"Cohen?" queried Arthur frowning, "You a Jewb... er, a Jew?"

"Yes, why?" asked Danny in surprise.

"Oh – er, nothing."

Danny looked at the tender already piled high with coal, "Well, how about getting some of the big lumps broken up, while I see to the fire?"

"I'd love to, but I injured my wrist this morning; tell you what, let me see to the gauges then you can forget them and just check the fire."

Danny looked surprised and then shrugged, "Fine by me."

He opened the fire doors to check the fire before adding, "But if you've injured your wrist, how can you fire on your next shift?"

Arthur had a quick answer, "Oh, I'm sure it'll be fine by then."

He began to check the gauges then turned to Ron, "What about you, Ron, are you Jewish as well?"

"No lad, I'm a Christian, and I'm not Ron to you, I'm Mr Smithers."

"Oh, yeah, sorry!" but he didn't sound sorry.

"How old are you?"

"Twenty two, why?"

"You were lucky to miss the call-up when the War broke out."

Arthur grinned. "No, not lucky, Mr Smithers; just smart."

"How come?"

"I was called up, but just before the medical, I went to see our local quack and slipped him ten bob; he gave me some pills which made my heart sound a bit dicky, so the army doc said I'd be no good. Then I joined the LMS as a cleaner and now I'm a passed cleaner. When I get to be a fireman, I'll be 'reserved occupation' and they can't call me up. I don't want a German bayonet in my belly. In any case, I don't reckon Hitler's as bad as they make out. He's got the right idea about the Commies an' the Jew... er... queers and some others."

"Mmmm," Ron was non-committal, "Well, check for the guard's flag, we should be off any moment now."

Arthur looked out back down the train, "We've got the 'right away', Mr Smithers," he called as they heard the guard's whistle.

Ron gently lifted the regulator and the train began to move off. Danny began to shovel, putting plenty of coal around the firebox so that the locomotive could have plenty of steam to bite on up the steep gradient out of Holyhead station. Many a train with an engine in poor condition had great difficulty in the climb out of Holyhead, and it wasn't unknown for a heavy express to stop half way up and send for a banker, but their big Scot took its fifteen corridors up the bank without any hesitation.

Their first stop was at Bangor and Danny, seeing an elderly man waiting on the platform, turned to Ron.

"Ron, there's old Jake Goldsmith; remember him? He used to be Head Porter here. I want to nip down for a quick word with him, I heard his missus was ill, won't be a jiffy."

"Righto Danny, but remember we're off in two minutes."

Danny nodded and climbed down to the platform and walked over to the old man.

Arthur sidled over to the driver.

"What's it like, Mr Smithers, having a Yid for a mate?" he asked quietly.

Ron stared at him for a moment, and then asked, "Who's your regular driver in Rhyl?"

"My driver?" asked Arthur in surprise, "His name is Ted Jones, why?"

"Next time you see him, give him my condolences."

"Condolences? What the hell for?" Arthur was clearly puzzled.

"For having you as a mate."

"Good news, Ron, Jake's old woman has recovered," said Danny as he climbed back into the cab, adding as he looked down the platform, "An' we've got the green."

"That's good, I liked old Jake," commented Ron as he gently lifted the regulator and the big engine began to move its heavy train out of the station. "During the great depression, he used to make the porters pool their tips and then make sure everyone got a share."

"What was his share?" asked Arthur.

"He didn't take a share; he said as Head Porter, he had a better wage than they did and could manage."

"But he collected all the tips, didn't he? So he could easily have taken a share without the others knowing."

"He could have, but he didn't; he just watched while the divvy was made in the porters' room."

"With a name like Jake Goldsmith, he could be Jewish."

"He *is* Jewish, so what?" asked Danny angrily.

"Oh... er, nothin'."

Danny grabbed his shovel, and rammed it into the tender and then swung it round to the firehole, making Arthur leap out of the way.

"Oi! Watch what you're doing!" yelled Arthur.

"I'm firing; it's my job," said Danny.

Ron smiled to himself as he watched out of the cab for the next set of signals.

Conversation in the cab lapsed for some time; it was clear that Arthur was not a welcome guest, although he kept a close eye on the gauges and warned Danny when the water needed replenishing.

After leaving Llandudno Junction, they picked up speed and Ron and Danny enjoyed the racing over the metals along the coast of North Wales as they passed the various resorts. However, shortly after passing Colwyn Bay, Ron was annoyed to see a distant signal at danger.

"What the bloody hell does the bobby think he's playing

at? We're supposed to have a clear run through to Rhyl!" he said angrily as he began to apply the brakes.

Enginemen running well always found an unexpected slowing or stopping highly frustrating. Reaching the next set of signals, they found the home signal also at red and they coasted to a stop.

"Must be a problem with the Denbigh freight crossing the down main," muttered Ron.

They waited for almost ten minutes until Ron turned to Arthur, "Get down to the signal box and find out what the bobby is playing at."

"It's a long way, and what about the gauges?" asked Arthur plaintively.

"Danny can deal with those; he usually does it anyway – it's his job," said Ron, getting impatient with his unwelcome passenger.

"Perhaps Danny could go, and I'll do a bit of firing?"

"Look, Arthur, you've got an injured wrist; a walk won't hurt it. Now hop it and find what the problem is and how long we'll have to wait here."

Grumbling to himself, Arthur climbed down to the track and began the long walk to the box which was at least half a mile away. He had been gone about five minutes when the home signal jerked upwards, giving them permission to continue. Ron lifted the regulator and the train moved slowly off again, picking up speed as they saw the next distant signal showing 'Clear'.

"Don't pick up too much speed, Ron, or Arthur won't be able to jump back on," advised Danny, then added mischievously, "Mind you, we're already going to be late into Rhyl and we might not be able to pick up enough to get into Chester right time. If we're late there we can't make up between there and Crewe."

"Yeah, that's a point," replied Ron thoughtfully. He eased the regulator up again, increasing speed. They passed a frantically waving Arthur at about 50 mph and accelerating.

"I feel sorry for Arthur," commented Danny, smiling as he shovelled coal into the firebox, "He's got a long walk into Abergele and even then he'll have to wait for the next stopper to Rhyl."

Ron looked at Danny in surprise, "You feel sorry for him? You don't look it."

Danny stood up and turned to Ron with an injured expression.

"Of course I feel sorry; as a good Jewish boy I even feel sorry for an offensive arsehole of a gentile!" he said indignantly, and bent back down to his firing, but the broad grin all over his face lasted for the rest of their shift.

14 - More foreign visitors (November 1943)

George and Lance were scheduled to run a Birkenhead parcels to Wellington.

As they approached the big 4-6-0 Grange class engine waiting for them in the shed, Lance commented, "You know, Mr D., I like these Granges; I reckon they've more guts than the Halls. I know they've smaller wheels, but they can belt along when they want to. And also, they forgive you if you make a cock-up, where a Hall wouldn't."

"Yes, I would normally agree, Lance," answered George, "But not perhaps in this case."

"Why?" asked Lance in surprise.

"This particular Grange badly needs attention; she's been on the road too long and is no longer reliable. We'll have to take care with her."

Before they climbed on board, the shed foreman called George into his office.

"I don't like the Grange you given us, Sid," said George, as he entered the office.

"No, George, I've been on to Wolverhampton Works for months to take her in for a 'sole and heel', but they always say they're too busy. Now, you're booked on the parcels to Wellington, then light engine to Wolverhampton, George, but not to Stafford Road. They want you at Oxley where you'll pick up a fitted freight to Aberystwyth, although you won't take it through. You detach at Salop and come back on a stopper to Chester."

"That's the official plan," Sid continued, and then walked to his door and shut it firmly. "Now I have a slightly different idea."

Sid proceeded to tell George what he wanted him to do.

"I see what you mean about this engine, Mr D.," said Lance as they pulled away from Chester General with the parcels, "She's takin' a lot of coal and not doin' much with it."

The engine's glands were leaking, one of the left hand cylinder cover bolts was dribbling, and, although Lance had checked the smoke-box door, it was clearly not airtight. George was having trouble with the regulator, which was loose, and one of the coupling rods clanked noisily. In short, the engine was in a bad way.

"Yes, if this were a Hall or a Castle, we'd have to fail it, but being a Grange, we might be able to keep her going," said George optimistically. Halfway up Gresford Bank there was a sudden *crack!* as the water gauge glass broke. Before any damage could be done however, Lance had replaced the glass with a spare which he carried with him, as all firemen were meant to.

They struggled to reach Wellington, where they pulled into the up slow platform.

George glanced out of the cab and commented, "Now there's a strange thing; a Southern train on the up main."

Lance leaned over to look out, "Yeah, looks like some sort of troop train."

They could see a train of green Southern Railway coaches and soldiers lined out on the platform behind a temporary fenced off area.

"Odd-looking uniforms they've got; they're grey," commented Lance.

"I know what it is; it's a POW train – they're German army. They're probably being sent to some prison camp in North Wales," said George, "I knew I'd seen those uniforms before, they're not very different from those in the last lot twenty-odd years back."

"The sods don't look much like the master race; half of 'em have no jackets or caps, their boots are dirty an' their lines are a bit ragged!" said Lance as he climbed down from the cab to uncouple the train. George sent him to get some drinking water from a tap on the platform; water from the tender, when boiled, was safe enough, but proper drinking water was always to be preferred if it could be easily obtained.

The pair sat drinking their tea while waiting for the line to Wolverhampton to clear for them. They listened with interest to the conversation on the platform between a limping British Army Major and a German officer who appeared to be in temporary charge of the thirty or so German soldiers guarded by half a dozen bored squaddies. The German officer marched up to the major, halted, and snapped off a smart salute.

"All present and correct, *Herr Leutnant*?" queried the major.

"One moment, sir, and I'll check."

The German turned to the double line of soldiers and barked, "*Achtung!*"

Every soldier stiffened and shuffled into straighter lines.

"*Stillgestanden!*"

Instantly, thirty pairs of heels clicked, the lines were now straight as a die and every head faced the front.

"Crikey!" Lance was impressed in spite of himself, "Their drill's bloody good!"

"Thank you, *Herr Leutnant*," said the major as he walked along, checking the numbers. "By the way, how come you speak such excellent English?"

"Thanks to two years in Cambridge, sir, from 1937 to '39. I trust when this lunacy between our two nations is over, I will be able to return and complete my degree."

"Well, the best of luck. OK, get your men back into the train."

The German soldiers climbed back into the train, which then moved off, leaving one of its coaches and another smaller group of a dozen Germans in similar uniforms but with the Waffen SS flash on their lapels. A small LMS tank engine approached, preparing to buffer up to the coach. The SS were carefully guarded by six British soldiers under the command of a hard-faced sergeant, all with rifles at the ready.

The major approached one of the Germans, who asked him, "And vot about us, *Herr* Major? Vhy ve not get back in ze train?"

"Well, like your people, *Scharführer*, we separate

branches of your forces into different camps. You Waffen SS are being sent to a camp in Scotland."

The man smiled thinly, "So? Not so easy to escape, *ja*? No matter, you Britishers cannot, how you say, to handle hard soldiers."

"I'm not sure I quite agree with you there. In any case the issue is irrelevant; the camp is not guarded by us. You'll be in the hands of the Norwegian Army."

The man's faced paled; one of his men muttered, "*Die Norweger! Scheisse!*"

"Errm... yes, quite," commented the major, trying to hide his grin. He looked over the Waffen SS soldiers once more, checking their number.

"Put 'em back into the coach, please, Sergeant," he said to the British sergeant, who waved the men back into the coach with his rifle.

Just as the SS were climbing into the coach, the small LMS tank engine opened its cylinder cocks with a *whoosh!* and covered everyone with a vast cloud of steam as it stopped.

When the steam had cleared, the sergeant shouted, "One o' the buggers is missin', sir!"

"He'll be hiding under the train, Sergeant," shouted the major, "Get a man at each end of the coach and another on the track round the back! We'll cut him off when he tries to break out. Don't shoot unless you have to."

"No!" George called over, "Leave him to us! We'll find him!"

Lance looked at George in surprise, "What? How do we do that?"

George pointed at the engine shed which was parallel to the up slow platform and right next to it. "Get a steam lance, lad! Quick!"

Lance grinned; "Oh yeah! That'll soon flush 'im out!"

A steam lance was normally used to clean out the tubes in a locomotive boiler, but it was clearly going to be put to an unusual use.

Lance raced across to the shed, grabbed a steam lance hose, ran to the front of their engine and attached the hose to the steam lance cock next to the smoke-box door. He hurried across the platform and aimed the nozzle of the hose under the train.

"Righto!" he called to George, and superheated steam shot from the hose.

There was a scream from under the train as the SS man scrambled out with his hands in the air; the sleeve of his right arm was steaming and his right hand had some skin peeling off it.

"Get one of your men to take him to the First Aid centre here in the station, Sergeant," said the major, unmoved, "And keep a close eye on him, though I don't think he's going to try and escape again for a while. I'll come and see to him, when the rest have gone."

The major then locked each door of the coach and the LMS tank engine drew the Southern coach back along the platform. It then attached the coach to the back of the Crewe train on the main down platform.

"Looks like they're heading north," said Lance, but George wasn't listening; he had climbed down and was chatting to the major on the platform.

"Are they really going to the Norwegians, or were you just scaring them?" he asked the major.

"Oh yes," replied the major, "I almost feel sorry for them. I was up at the camp in Scotland three months back to give the Norwegians a copy of our manual for dealing with POWs. Their colonel said, 'Thank you Major, but I don't need it. I only escaped from Trondheim myself four months ago. I found the regular German Army soldiers mostly just wanted to get back home, but the Waffen SS troops are, er - what is your English expression - a different pot of fish? And I am very much looking forward to handling them.'"

The major continued, "That colonel wouldn't even let me look round the camp, 'in case you notice anything which you feel you would have to report to your superiors. This would cause no end of embarrassment and paperwork for everyone.'"

Lance leaned out of the cab and said, "But aren't the

Norwegians our allies? They're not thugs, are they?"

The major glanced up at him, "Generally no, they're pretty fair-minded; obviously they resent the regular German army and want it out of their country, but they loathe the Waffen SS and they're understandably keen to - err - even the balance, I suppose you might say."

George nodded, "Yes, I was a corporal in the Great War and we thought the ordinary Jerries were pretty much the same as us - just on the wrong side. But there was no Nazism then, of course."

In the meantime, the porters and Post Office officials had nearly completed unloading the parcels.

George pulled out his watch from his jacket, glanced at it, and said to Lance, "Almost time to head off again. Have you checked everything?"

Before Lance could answer, the major turned to George again. "When the War broke out, you didn't want to go back into the Army?"

"My wishes didn't come into it, Major; I was too old, and anyway, as Lance and I were already engine crew, we weren't permitted to volunteer. Young Lance here tried to pull a trick on the boss; he applied for the Army and waited until the boss had a lot of papers to sign and pushed it in the bottom of the pile, but the boss saw it and refused to sign. 'Reserved Occupation, Lance, my lad,' he said, 'I'm not losing you to the Army.'"

"Ah yes, of course," commented the major. "Well, good luck!" With that he limped off down the platform.

By this time the signal had dropped to clear the up main to Wolverhampton. George eased up the regulator and the engine moved off. Not having any train, the engine moved much more easily, and their run to Oxley shed at Wolverhampton was more relaxing, although there was a consistent clanking from the loose coupling rod.

At Oxley they headed straight for the turntable so they could turn the engine before taking it to the coaling stage.

George slowed the engine right down to walking pace, "Hop off, Lance, and get the bridge table ready."

Lance jumped off, ran to the turntable bridge, and began to push it to line up with the approach road.

There was a dull thump under the engine, and George shot his head out of the cab:

"Lance!" he shouted urgently, "Look out! The brake's gone!"

George turned quickly to the tender handbrake but it jammed and the locomotive trundled slowly and remorselessly towards the turntable well. As Lance hadn't been able to line up the table in time, the engine dipped its front bogie and tipped into the well with George clutching on to the cab handrail as the cab rose into the air. There were vast clouds of steam from both cylinders as the covers burst open.

A crowd gathered quickly around the stricken engine and the angry shed foreman ran over.

"What the hell? George?" the foreman cried in shock, as he recognized the driver. "How on earth could you of all people make such a bloody stupid mistake?"

"The engine brake failed and the damn tender handbrake jammed. There was nothing I could do to stop her!" growled George indignantly.

"Well Chester shed won't be happy with you – this engine of yours is going to have to go into the Works, and Sid will be an engine short for several weeks! I wouldn't like to be in your shoes when you get back!"

On the way home, George and Lance had an elderly Dean Goods on the Aberystwyth goods as far as Salop and changed to a 43xx mixed traffic engine on the Chester stopper.

Lance glanced several times curiously at his driver as they returned to their home shed, but the latter seemed to have nothing on his conscience. At Chester, as they were leaving after their shift, the shed foreman headed towards them.

Lance began to feel distinctly uneasy, until Sid shook

George by the hand, saying, "I've just had the Oxley shed foreman on the phone, George; thanks very much, I owe you one!"

On their way out, Lance could not control his curiosity, "Mr D., you wreck one of 'is engines, an' he thanks yer for it! What the 'ell's all that about?"

George grinned at his fireman. "You're a good lad, Lance, but you've still got a bit to learn. Ever heard the expression, 'Ask no questions and you get no lies?'"

15 - You can't win them all! (January 1944)

There was thick snow on the ground as Driver George Denton and his fireman Lance Hargreaves walked into Chester Shed to report for duty. They were both well wrapped up against the cold, Driver Denton with his smart overcoat and leather gloves and Lance wearing an ex-Army greatcoat and a pair of woollen gloves which had seen many better days.

"Jeez, Mr D., I'll be glad to get into the enginemen's cabin," commented Lance as they crossed the tracks to the main locomotive shed.

"Yes, well go and see what Sid's got lined up for us today, Lance," answered George as he stopped to look at three fitters working on a large Castle class 4-6-0 up on the hoist and which was missing its two front driving wheels.

"I feel sorry for those three poor devils out here in the weather; at least we'll be in a warm cab," he continued.

Lance came into the enginemen's cabin a few minutes later and stared at George, who had his hands round a hot mug of tea.

"What's up, Lance? Why are you looking at me like that?" the driver asked.

"Mr Thomson's given us a double home turn!"

A double home turn meant that they would have to stay away overnight because the shift involved a long distance which wouldn't allow a return home in the time allotted.

"A double home? He can't do that without warning us!" said George angrily, "What's he playing at? I'll go and see him now. Er - what's the shift?"

"Heavy Salop stopper and then ECS to Bristol, back the next day."

"Must be some emergency; Sid wouldn't do that otherwise."

George left the cabin to return five minutes later, nodding sadly. "Yes, apparently somebody in Plymouth wants empty coaches by tonight and Crewe has some spare; they'll send them to Salop where we'll pick them up."

George and Lance picked up their Hall class engine, backed across the station throat on to the twelve coaches in Platform Two, and Lance coupled the engine to the coaches while George filled in the details of the train journal.

The driver looked down the platform as Lance climbed back into the cab.

"We might have a bit of trouble starting today," George commented, "The train is very full and the snow is making the rails wet. She might pick up her heels as we move out."

Sure enough, as George eased the heavy load out of the platform, and they came out of the overall roofing to meet the wet rails, the engine's driving wheels lost adhesion and there was an almighty roar as all the wheels spun round before George could lower the regulator. The spinning slowed, Lance manipulated the sand levers, which squirted sand from the sand pipes under the wheels, and George tried again but with the same result: another thunderous roar and the wheels spun again.

"The bloody sand's wet!" called Lance.

"Try again," said George, lowering the regulator once more. Lance fired more sand under the wheels and this time they took hold and the train slowly increased its speed.

George took the train gently round to the left on to the LMS down slow line through the two tunnels under the Northgate CLC station and gradually accelerated past the canal and under the City Walls (here Lance kept an eye open for schoolboys and their snowballs) and past the racecourse. By the time they were across the Dee Bridge, they were moving at a comfortable rate and slowing down slightly for Saltney Junction where they had a down grade when they entered the GWR metals.

As they slowed down to stop at the little station at Saltney, Lance noticed a girl waiting at the end of the wooden platform and, although she was wrapped up in a heavy, pale green overcoat, she looked very attractive. Lance gave her a close examination as they passed and watched to see which compartment she climbed into.

"You checking the water, Lance?" asked George sharply as he saw that Lance was inattentive to his work.

"What? Oh, yeah," replied Lance, pulling his head inside the cab quickly.

"Pretty girl out there?"

"No, I was watching a porter with a heavy case," said Lance.

"Nice legs, had she?"

"Geez yes," said Lance, "An' 'er hair was..? Er... who, the porter?"

George chuckled, "You'll never change, lad! Now see if we've got the green."

While standing at Wrexham, Lance heard a girl's voice calling up to the cab and he looked out and saw the pretty girl on the platform.

"Er... excuse me Driver, where does this train go to?"

"Salop," he answered, "We'll be there in about an hour and a half."

"Oh dear!" said the girl, "I was sure the train went to Shrewsbury."

"Sorry!" replied Lance with a smile, "Don't worry. Enginemen all call Shrewsbury Salop; don't know why. So you'll be right."

"Oh thank you, that's a relief,"

"Goin' fer a day trip?" he asked.

"No, I have an aunt who's a bit poorly, I'm going to stay with her tonight to see that she's looked after. My uncle's away till tomorrow."

"Goin' home tomorrow?" Lance was suddenly interested.

"Yes, on an afternoon train."

"Might see you again and we could..."

An angry call came from the other side of the cab, "Oi Lance! What's the delay?"

"Sorry Mr D.," Lance looked down the platform to see the guard frantically waving his green flag, "We've got the green."

He stuck his head out of the cab quickly and gestured urgently to the girl to get back into her coach.

"Just a passenger with a question," Lance said to George as he opened the firehole ready to shovel more coal in, "Wanted to check that we were for Salop."

"Hmmmh!" muttered his driver, unsure of what Lance had been doing. "Just make sure you keep your mind on the job!"

George studied Lance's face but couldn't decide whether to chide his fireman further. Lance's face gave nothing away, so George pulled the whistle chain and concentrated on getting the Hall away again in the rain, without slipping.

They arrived punctually in Shrewsbury. Lance tried to catch another glimpse of the girl. However, George sent him to the engine smokebox to add a headlamp to the right hand buffer beam, changing from that of a stopping train; a single headlamp at the top of the smokebox, to that of an empty coaching stock.

A porter walked along the platform calling "All change!" as the passengers all disembarked.

An inspector was waiting near the cab.

"You're ECS to Bristol, and the LMS coaches are over in the bay," he said to George.

George looked over to see six red LMS coaches, and he turned back and stared at the official.

"Six bogies?" he queried. "We've already got twelve on; are we leaving some of them here?"

The inspector scratched his head and checked his list.

"No," he said, shaking his head, "They're all to go to Bristol where you'll be relieved."

"But eighteen 35-tonners? We've only got this Hall and –

oh, I see, we're getting a pilot engine?"

"Pilot? Nothing here about double heading; I doubt whether the Coleham shedmaster has a spare engine anyway. Sorry – they're all yours!"

With that, the inspector left.

In the meantime, Lance had returned. He had a satisfied smile on his face; the pretty girl had been late leaving her compartment and Lance had managed a quick word with her.

"What have you got to smile at?" growled George, glaring at him.

"Me? Oh nuthin'!"

"Well I've got some news that'll wipe that smile off your face!" George was unusually short-tempered. "We're to pick up those six LMS coaches and take them with our lot to Temple Meads."

Lance stared at his driver, "What? Eighteen coaches with a Hall?"

"All eighteen!"

"Are they givin' us a pilot engine?"

"No pilot!" George sighed, "Sorry Lance, you're going to have to work very hard between here and Bristol. The road is hilly and we've got a savage load; at least the coaches are empty – that'll help."

"But a Hall? Will she handle the load?"

"She won't like it, that's for sure, but fortunately she's in good nick and we might make it. If we get really stuck, we'll have to call on Hereford for a pilot."

Lance groaned, "What about me back? I'll be shovellin' the whole damn way!"

"Well it'll take your mind off that girl you were chatting up; I know why you took so long to change the headlamps! In any case, I'll do the firing for you between Leominster and Hereford to give you a break."

"Ta Mr D., that'd be a great help."

"I might even give you a hand when we're climbing up out of the Severn Tunnel."

"Crikey! I'd forgotten about that tunnel – it's a bloody

steep climb out!"

"It'll make you sleep well in the railwaymen's digs in Bristol too; you won't even want to check out the local talent!"

The shift became a nightmare for Lance; he was a fit young man as well as being a competent fireman, but this trip was by far the hardest he had ever had in five years of firing. George took over the firing twice to give him a break; even so, the constant firing, bringing the coal forward onto the shovelling plate, dipping the scoop into the water troughs, plus all the other duties that were expected of a fireman, rendered Lance totally exhausted by the time they pulled in at Temple Meads.

The relief fireman couldn't believe his eyes when he glanced into the tender; it was almost empty.

"Didn't they give you any coal?" he demanded, "This'll not get us to Plymouth!"

"We left Chester with an overflowing tender," snapped Lance, "An' we didn't get a chance to top up. Then we left Salop with eighteen bogies, so you'll 'ave to take 'er under the coal drop at Bath Road yourselves if you want to go any further in 'er today!"

With this parting shot, Lance climbed wearily from the cab.

A short time later in the overnight digs, their landlady offered them a cup of tea, but Lance merely shook his head and went straight to bed.

"You'll have to excuse my mate," George said to the landlady, "He's not usually like that – he's had a very heavy day."

The following day at Bath Road shed, the word of George and Lance's achievement of the previous day had got around. They were cheered as they entered the enginemen's cabin for duty.

The shed foreman came over and said to them, "After what you blokes did yesterday, I can hardly give a normal shift so I've got a light goods for Hereford for you – shouldn't

118

require any heavy work."

"Much appreciated!" replied George, "I don't think my mate here could manage anything solid today!"

They went out to collect their engine, a 2-6-0 mogul, and backed her onto their light goods which consisted of twenty empty open wagons plus the brake van. Their engine was in reasonable condition and they pulled out past a set of sidings cut by a large crater, five open wagons rendered into matchwood and two pannier tanks with tarpaulins over them.

"Looks like the Luftwaffe was here again recently," commented George to Lance.

The light load provided a fairly easy run to Hereford where the shedmaster sent them on the cushions to Salop.

"We might get lucky again and get back all the way home on the cushions again, Lance," said George.

To his surprise, Lance said, "Or we could take the 2.17 back to Chester; after the comfy ride from Hereford, I reckon I could manage a bit o' shovellin' again."

"You want to fire again?"

"Gotta keep fit," said Lance, flexing his arm muscles.

George frowned and then smiled.

"You've got to keep fit for that girl!" he laughed, "I bet she said she'd be on the 2.17!"

"What girl's this then, Mr D.?" asked Lance, all innocence.

The Coleham shedmaster was pleased to accept their offer to take the Chester train even though the Salop crew on it had not completed their shift; it gave him more leeway to use them elsewhere. George and Lance saw with pleasure their engine was a Castle in reasonable condition as they mounted the cab when it stopped at Platform Three.

George looked along the platform as he climbed up and saw a girl in a light green coat talking to a burly young man who seemed angry about something. She got into a compartment while the young man strode purposefully along the platform towards the engine.

George turned to Lance, who was busily checking the gauges. "Lance, get along the offside running plate and check that we've got express headlamps on the smokebox."

Lance turned in surprise, "Express headlamps? Why should I check those? They'll've been put on at Wolverhampton!"

"*Now*, Lance!" George used a tone that Lance knew well – it brooked no argument, "And stay on the offside until I tell you to return to the cab!"

Lance stared at George, and without a word climbed out of the cab then moved along to the smokebox of the engine.

In the meantime, the young man had reached the cab and stared up at George.

"Are you the bastard who tried to chat up my girl?" he snarled, "I'm coming up to have a word."

George leaned out of his cab. "Entry to my cab is by invitation only," he replied, "And you're not invited."

The young man grabbed the handrail to pull himself up the steps. As he reached the top step, he found the sharp, polished steel edge of a shovel directly under his chin. He paused and saw the driver holding the shovel firmly.

"I served in the First War," said George conversationally, "And we found that if you lost your rifle, an entrenching spade made a good alternative; you could take a man's head off with it."

The young man remained on the top step, looked carefully at George and said, "It wasn't you, was it? It was your young mate."

He began to climb down the steps again, "Tell him I'll be waiting for him in Chester!"

With that he walked back down the train.

"You can come back now, Lance," called George and Lance climbed back into the cab from the offside running plate. His face was pale.

"I don't think I want him sortin' me out in Chester!" he said, glancing down the train at the figure disappearing into a compartment, "'E's like a bloody gorilla; the bugger must be a yard across the shoulders!"

The run to Chester was uneventful, but as they drew up in Number Three bay, George said, "Now nip out and uncouple, and then I want you to..."

He told Lance what he was to do. Lance nodded and

scrambled down to the track to uncouple. There was a gentle nudge as a big Prairie at the other end of the train backed on in preparation for taking the train back out and on to Birkenhead.

"Now, where's that mate of yours?" came a loud, angry voice from the platform.

George looked out to see the girl and her young gorilla waiting on the platform.

"I know he's hiding up there somewhere – he has to keep the fire for you, so I'll have the sod this time!"

George gestured for the young man to climb into the cab, which he did with alacrity. In the cab, George pointed to the steam pressure gauge which showed 60 pounds, and then he opened the firebox and pointed at the fire which was very low.

"I don't need a fireman now," he said, "This engine has finished its turn – it's going on shed; I have enough steam to take it across to the shed."

"Well, where is he?" demanded the angry young man, "I want to teach him not to try and chat up any girl he fancies."

George took the young man by the shoulder and pointed to the tail end of the train disappearing in the distance. "You'll have to rush; his shift hasn't finished and he's now firing to the driver of the Birkenhead."

As the frustrated young man walked along the platform to his girlfriend and the exit, a shaking Lance climbed back into the cab from the offside running plate.

"Thanks a million, Mr D., you've saved my bacon!" he said.

"One day, Lance my lad, I won't be here to save your bacon," commented George, easing the regulator in preparation for the starting signal, "And if you haven't learned by then that not every girl is fair game, you're going to get yourself sorted good and proper!"

For once in his life, Lance was at a loss for words.

16 - The American Flyer (April 1944)

By early 1944, in some ways life had become safer for most enginemen, with far fewer air attacks on railway property, but this was counterbalanced by other problems.

After five years of war, railway maintenance had suffered badly. However, like everyone else in the country, railway authorities had learned to make do: engines that in peacetime would have been sent to Wolverhampton or Swindon for regular maintenance were given only temporary repairs; older engines that should have been scrapped long ago were still running; trackwork needed attention, and a myriad other matters that made the system safe could not always be attended to. All this meant that the job was not getting easier.

Food shortages were another problem. It was all very well for the older drivers to claim that if you were held up at a signal for a few minutes then bacon and eggs fried on the fireman's shovel in the firebox tasted quite magnificent; but after years of severe rationing, you couldn't easily get either. At least tea was still relatively easy to get, so a brew-up was often possible.

George Denton and Lance Hargreaves were on an unusual run; this morning they were taking a 43xx class 2-6-0 light engine to Manchester. The Manchester to North Wales passenger trains were normally headed by LMS engines but the GWR had running powers to Manchester via Warrington and occasionally used them.

On this occasion, Patricroft shed near Manchester had been on the receiving end of a raid and a number of its engines had been damaged. The Great Western had offered to send a light engine to Manchester to bring a North Wales train back as far as Chester, where the LMS shed could take over.

On their way north, their light engine was briefly stopped at the Helsby starter signal; they saw an American soldier waving to them from the platform. He came over as Lance looked down from the cab.

"Hey buddy, you couldn't take me to Padgate could you? I'd sure be grateful."

George came over next to Lance and answered, "Sorry mate, we don't go to Padgate, but we can get you to Warrington, if that's any help."

The American smiled, swung himself up into the cab and introduced himself, "Major Lewis B. Walker, USAAF, at your service. I'm real grateful to you guys."

"The pleasure's all ours," said George, "With you fellows helping us, we can't lose this damn war!"

Major Walker was impeccably dressed in his neat green uniform, and Lance said curiously, "Our Air Force blokes are in blue uniforms; why are yours green?"

"We're actually American Army, but our airmen are green to distinguish from our soldiers who are khaki like your army guys. By the way, you won't get into trouble giving me a lift in your cab, will you? I wouldn't want you to get into any problems on my account."

"Well, Control doesn't like us giving lifts, but we'll be in Warrington in about twenty minutes. You will have to watch out for your uniform though; a locomotive cab isn't the cleanest of places, and," added George, "You might have to jump at Warrington if the line is clear; we can't stop, but we'll slow down for you."

"Well I'm mighty glad you can help me. The guys in the station said the next train's not due for another three hours, and I have to fly a B-17 today and be at the briefing in two hours. My jeep broke down coming through Helsby so I thought I might take a train. I can call the Army at Warrington and they'll send a car."

"So where are you flying to?" asked Lance.

The major laughed, "Germany, I guess, but that's classified information!"

"Oh yeah, sorry," said Lance, abashed, "I forgot!"

They were catching up to a goods train ahead of them

and they were slowed down at Frodsham distant signal. Lance checked the fire and as he was satisfied with it he reached for his lunch box.

The major watched him take out a sandwich, and said curiously, "What's in that sandwich?"

Lance opened it up and showed him.

"Bread and marge with jam," he said, "Me mum got our jam ration yesterday."

"That light pink smear – that's jam?"

"Yeah, why?"

The major shook his head in disbelief, "And that's a treat?"

"Yeah, we don't always get jam, sometimes it's just dripping."

"Dripping? What's dripping?"

"It's the fat from the meat we cook; it's left in the pan, so we scrape it out and put it on sandwiches with a bit of salt."

"Mmmmh..." said the major thoughtfully, "It's no wonder you Limeys are all so thin!"

The American was good company for the next fifteen minutes as they ran towards Warrington, then George said, "We're nearly there, Major, and the distant signal is clear, so we can't stop. Lance, make some heavy smoke so they'll think we've got a problem; then they won't be surprised if they see us slow down."

As Lance found some duff coal to put into the firebox, the major got ready to climb down the cab steps.

"Hey! Where are you guys based?" he called.

"Chester, Great Western," answered George. 'Why?"

"Thanks buddies!"

The major dropped off neatly onto the platform as they trundled through. They saw him wave as he hurried towards the platform exit.

"Nice bloke," commented Lance as he shovelled some better coal into the firebox. The rest of the run to Patricroft was uneventful and they turned and serviced the engine before running tender-first up to Manchester Exchange to back onto the North Wales passenger.

On their run back to Chester with the Llandudno express, George remarked, "I'll bet that Yank is flying his B-17 on an air raid today. I hope he makes it back safely. The Americans often fly in daylight so they're easier targets for Jerry fighters."

"Yeah, he's a brave fellah, and... oh!"

"What?" asked George.

"Problem – I meant to go fer a piss at Patricroft an' forgot."

"So? We'll be in Chester in thirty minutes."

"I can't wait thirty minutes."

"Why on Earth didn't you go at Exchange?"

"I was busy couplin' up and that," answered Lance

"How can you forget to go for a pee?"

"I dunno, I just did."

"Well pee on the coal in the tender – and make sure you shovel that bit of coal into the firebox damn quickly."

George turned and looked out of the cab; he was fastidious and didn't want to see his fireman deal with his problem. He only turned back to the regulator when he heard Lance shovelling coal vigorously.

"Feel better now?"

"Yeah," said Lance, relieved.

"Cleaned the shovel?"

"Yep."

"If you ever do that again in my cab, you'll pay for it, young fellah; I'll have my regulator up and tear great holes out of your fire, and you'll be shovelling a ton every ten miles!"

"Sorry, Mr D."

"You would be. Now keep your eyes peeled for the Frodsham distant; it should be coming up very soon."

A week later, as George and Lance were coming off their shift, they saw a familiar figure waiting by the shed gate. It was their major from the USAAF.

"You guys got a coupla hours to spare?" he greeted them. "I'd like to take you for a little run in my jeep."

"Hello Major, good to see you," said George with a

smile. "We're glad to see you survived your flying."

"I'd have to tell me mum, I'll be late," said Lance.

"Yes, I should warn my missus too," said George, "She'll worry otherwise."

"OK, hop in and we'll drive round and let your folks know you'll be late."

"Where are we goin'?" asked Lance.

"You'll find out soon," responded the major with a chuckle.

He drove them both to their respective homes to inform their womenfolk about their trip to the unknown, and then set off with them on the Warrington road.

"I'm taking you guys on a little trip to Padgate," explained Major Walker, "You might like to see how Uncle Sam looks after his soldiers."

As they neared the centre of Padgate, they saw many American uniforms on the streets.

"Will yer look at that, Mr D.!" said Lance in disbelief. On a busy street corner in the centre of the town were two American military policemen standing side by side, watching the passers-by. They were smartly attired with white webbing belts, gaiters and lanyards; both were standing identically with their legs 'at ease', peaked caps at exactly the same angle.

"They're chewin' gum," laughed Lance, "An' even their bloody chins are movin' up and down in time!"

They drove past a large military base and Major Walker said, "That's where I live, but I can't take visitors inside. We're going next door."

He stopped the jeep outside a gigantic warehouse and said, "I'll need a hand in here."

George and Lance got out and followed him inside. He said something to a soldier at a desk, who pointed to a nearby door. Nodding his thanks, Major Walker waved the two enginemen to follow him and went into a small room. There were four largish cardboard boxes on the floor.

"These are mine," he said, "They go in the jeep."

They loaded the boxes into the jeep, and got back in.

"I owe you guys a drink," said Major Walker, "I'm not

126

allowed to take you on our base to the PX, so we'll go to a pub I know of."

He pulled up at a small pub and they all went inside. The range of drinks on a shelf behind the bar was unusually large for a wartime pub.

"We help the barman out with his supplies occasionally," explained the major, "Two double whiskies, Harry, and a soda for me, I'm on stand-by."

Lance shook George's arm urgently, and hissed in his ear, "Mr D., I can't afford to stand a round of drinks like this; I'm skint!"

"Been seeing Rosie again, have you?" whispered George back.

Major Walker overheard them and said, "Gee, I should have warned you; you aren't members of this bar, you aren't allowed to pay for drinks. They're on me tonight!"

After a couple more beers, the major said it was time to get back. They piled cheerfully into his jeep and he drove them back to Chester.

They stopped outside Lance's house, but before Lance could thank the American, the latter pointed to two of the boxes and said, "Lance, take those with you and give them to your Mom with my compliments."

He turned to George and said, "The other two, George, are for your wife; she may find the contents of interest."

"Many thanks, Major," said George, "You've given my fireman and me a real treat we won't forget in a hurry."

"The thanks is all on my side, George," said the major, "You guys got me out of a bad situation last week at some risk to your jobs. You helped me plenty!"

With that he took George home and gave a cheery wave as he departed back to his base.

Next morning, Lance, hearing a knock, opened his door and was very surprised to see his driver standing there.

"Morning Mr Denton; is there a problem?"

"No, Lance, but there might be. Are you ready?"

"Yep, I'll just get me lunch box."

"Ah yes, your lunch box, we need to talk about that on

the way to the shed."

On their way, George said, "No doubt you investigated the contents of your boxes last night?"

"Did we what!" said Lance with enthusiasm, "Me mum couldn't believe it! Butter, peanut butter, real coffee, packets of Jello – what's Jello anyway? - strawberry jam, tins of ham, chocolate, sweets an'..."

"Yes, we got the lot too," interrupted George, "But I want you to keep quiet about all that; if the others knew about it they'd all be stopping and trying to pick up Yanks, instead of concentrating on their jobs. We wouldn't be doing the Americans any favours."

"Yeah, I see what you mean," said Lance thoughtfully, "OK, I'll keep me gob shut."

"That would be a good idea."

Their shift that day was a shunting turn, an easy duty with a 57xx class 0-6-0 tank engine, but George puzzled Lance immensely when he drove the engine onto the turntable.

"What do we need to turn for?" he demanded, "This is a tank engine!"

"We're not turning," said George, "We're just going over the table and on to the long siding."

"Yeah, but why?" Lance couldn't understand his driver.

George stopped the engine just short of the buffers on the isolated siding and screwed down the handbrake.

"What have you got for lunch?" he asked.

"I thought I'd have me a peanut butter sandwich."

"Good heavens, you even sound like a Yank. I'm also trying a ham sandwich. And I bet you're going to drink some coffee."

"Yeah, well why not?"

"Tell me Lance, what did we talk about on the way to work this morning?"

"About keeping stumm about them American goodies."

"Exactly. And that's why we're eating here. I want to enjoy my first cup of real coffee in five years without having all the blokes sniffing round like er..."

"Like flies round shit."

"Lance, you have a regrettably coarse vocabulary, but you're dead right."

And George settled himself comfortably on his tip-up seat, sniffed appreciatively at his mug of coffee and bit with long-awaited relish into his ham sandwich.

17 - The doodlebug (June 1944)

In general, things were looking up on some fronts; the Americans had begun to make their presence felt and the Allies had landed in Occupied France two weeks previously and were beginning to move deeper, having apparently caught the German Army by surprise.

Food shortage was, of course, still an issue, but at least the general public could now foresee an end to the War and could begin to look forward to an end to rationing.

Railway maintenance, however, was an increasing problem as engines were kept on long past their scrapping dates and newer locomotives were often built and put into harness without adequate testing. Consequently, life in the cabs was not all beer and skittles, although attacks on trains by low flying Messerschmidts were now rare, as the RAF controlled British skies in daylight.

However, London, Birmingham, Manchester, Liverpool, Plymouth and other major cities still occasionally suffered night-time raids by enemy bombers. While the Blackout still held firm in the country, causing inconvenience to railwaymen, especially those involved in night shunting, as well as frequent road accidents for the general public, people were beginning to relax regarding the bombing as the sound of air raid sirens became less common. Naturally, people were fed up with the constraints put upon them by the War, but there was no doubt that an element of optimism was creeping into life in Britain.

For George and Lance too, there were some improvements. Lance, now Fireman Hargreaves, was taking on a greater share of the driving and George found himself feeling far more at ease when Lance was on the regulator. Their teamwork was beginning to make a name for itself in their home shed as in other sheds in the Wolverhampton Division. They were often scheduled for some of the more difficult trains, and putting in overtime was a healthy way of adding to their bank accounts (especially as Lance had decided that the financial burden of his visits to Lime Street was no longer acceptable).

One day in early July, as they were walking to the shed on their morning shift, George asked Lance to make sure he could bring a second set of clean clothes to work the following day.

"Wot for?" Lance wanted to know.

"Not sure yet, but Sid mentioned the possibility of a fairly dirty coal train job tomorrow down as far as Wellington before we bring the Birkenhead back from Wolverhampton. If you climb into the cab at Stafford Road all filthy, you won't feel right for the rest of the shift."

"So I 'ave to shovel coal into a Castle or Star cab wearin' a nice clean overall?"

"Look Lance, you're getting to be a good fireman; I'm trying to turn you into a Passed Fireman so that you can in turn become a Driver. It's not all just knowing how to keep the water boiled and the steam pressure up. There's much more to it than that; it helps to look the part as well."

Lance thought about this. "You mean I should try and keep me clobber a bit cleaner?"

"Among other things, yes."

"Wot other things?"

"Well for example, you could try and tone down your language."

"You mean not swearin' an' that?"

"It would help."

"Mmmm... I'll see if I can change me speakin' 'abits."

George sighed; it wasn't going to be easy, but the lad had great promise.

The shift next day was not the dirty coal train they expected; apparently it had been rerouted via Crewe and they took the up Margate as far as Wolverhampton as usual.

"Needn't 'ave brought me clean gear," grumbled Lance

as they climbed down from the cab in Stafford Road shed and walked to the enginemen's cabin.

After eating their sandwiches they strolled over to where their engine stood ready to be taken to the station to pick up the Birkenhead express.

"Crikey! Look at that!" Lance was startled to see the Star class engine; it was immaculate and gleaming with its shining Brunswick green paint, fully lined out, and even had its buffers polished. Lance hadn't seen anything like it in the last five years. As they climbed into the spotless cab they saw a locomotive inspector already waiting.

"Morning George; this is Fireman Hargreaves?"

"Yes, Harry," said George, "That's him."

The inspector shook Lance by the hand. "I'm Inspector Lynton, Hargreaves, I'll be accompanying you as far as Gobowen."

"Yessir; er, why? An' why the clean engine?"

"We've got a Royal coming to Oswestry today, and she's on the 11.10 from Paddington, the two coaches to be detached at Gobowen. I'm glad you keep your overalls clean, that's not easy for a fireman; it looks so much better and will be noted on your record."

Lance glanced at George who stared back at him, unblinking.

They backed the engine into the Great Western Low-Level station at Wolverhampton and waited on one of the centre down roads until the Birkenhead train, headed by an equally gleaming and spotless King class, pulled in to the platform. After a few moments' delay, the King eased forward with six coaches to the carriage sidings, leaving the rest of the train for George and Lance's Star to back on. The guard came to inform them that their train had ten corridors; a heavier load than usual. The two extra were at the rear for the Royal party and staff.

"We've got some coal all nicely broken up, but I 'ope the engine's in good nick," muttered Lance to George as they waited for the guard's whistle.

"Don't worry, Lance, she'll have been thoroughly checked out by the fitters, and in any case, Salop will

132

have a spare engine ready in an emergency."

Lance leaned out of the cab and stared back down the platform. "'Ere we go, Mr D. I can see the guard's green flag!"

George pulled the whistle chord and lifted the regulator gently but firmly. The engine began to glide smoothly away with its train.

The locomotive inspector looked at Lance and said, "You can see why they picked Mr Denton for this job can't you, Fireman Hargreaves?"

Without waiting for an answer, he turned to George, "And how about your fireman, George? Will he manage, or will I have to roll my sleeves up?"

"Don't you worry, Harry, Lance may only be a young 'un, but he knows how to keep the steam pressure up so I can use it."

Their run to Gobowen was smoothly accomplished, with stops at Wellington and Shrewsbury. Officials were waiting anxiously on the platforms as they drew in to each station. Inspector Lynton was able to reassure them that everything was under control and there was no need to call upon any spare engine or engine crew.

Nearing Gobowen, the express was held briefly at a signal short of the station while an immaculate 45xx class 2-6-2 light tank engine drew the two Royal coaches off the back of the train and then departed south with its load down the short branch to Oswestry. The main train stopped in the station for the normal passengers to join the little push-pull auto which was waiting to follow the Royal train on the last mile or so into Oswestry. In the Star cab, Inspector Lynton made a few notes into a small notebook he carried, turned to George and Lance and thanked them for their efforts then descended to the platform.

"That's a feather in your cap, Lance," said George later as they took the train towards Ruabon, "Harry Lynton is a stickler for getting things ship-shape and Bristol fashion. He was pleased with you."

"Why didn't you tell me we was workin' a Royal?"

"I didn't know for sure."

"I could've forgot me clean clobber!"

"Time you learned the finer points of being a Great Western engineman. You'll be taking your driving exam one day."

"Well, ta anyway. Tell yer what – let me buy you a pint or two in the Wheatsheaf after the shift; you did push me to get me clean gear."

"Thanks Lance, that's a nice gesture, but only a couple of pints – we're on again tomorrow, remember"

"I see; Passed Fireman is OK, pissed fireman is not. Yeah, OK, two pints it is."

A week later, the two of them found themselves on a long, heavy freight heading towards London. Their engine, an elderly 2-8-0, was managing the job but it was hard work. Both men were looking forward to their arrival in Acton Yard and then travelling on the cushions in a local train to the comfort of a bed in the railwaymen's lodge near Old Oak Common.

They had drawn into the main up arrival loop and Lance climbed down to uncouple the wagons while a 57xx 0-6-0 Pannier coupled on to the guard's van at the other end to begin dividing the train. After Lance had completed the job, he walked to where George had climbed down from the cab of the 2-8-0 and they had begun to walk towards the station when they heard an odd rumbling sound in the sky. They both looked up to see a strange, small aircraft flying quite low towards them.

"What the 'ell's that?" asked Lance, "Never seen one o' them before."

Suddenly, the rumbling sound cut out and the aircraft began to tumble out of the sky.

"Whatever it is, the pilot's got a big problem!" shouted George, "Come on Lance, he's going to crash near us and we might be able to help!"

They both began to run to where they thought the aircraft might land. It dropped about a hundred yards away in a nearby field and exploded with a huge flash and a roar. Both men were flung back several yards; neither got up again.

Two days later, George woke up in bed. It was dark, and he could hear a rustling sound. He tried to sit up, but found he was too weak. He felt a bandage round his head.

"Who's that? And where am I?"

"Ah, Mr Denton, you're awake." The woman's voice was pleasant. "Just relax; you're in hospital and you've had a bit of a bump on the head. Nothing to worry about. I'll let the doctor know you're awake and he will come and explain in a few minutes."

"What happened? Why do I have a bandage round my eyes?"

"It was apparently a plane crash, but we're not quite sure how it happened."

"How is my fireman, Lance Hargreaves?"

"Er... he's rather more badly hurt, but the doctor will tell you more than I can."

"How badly? He's not..?"

"No, he will live, but his injuries are severe; but I can't tell how severe. Just try and relax, and I will go and call the doctor for you."

She patted his pillow and settled him down again. He heard the rustle of her skirt as she left.

Shortly after, George heard another set of heavier footsteps and a man's voice.

"Mr Denton, I'm so glad you're back with us; you've had a very near squeak. I also think you've been very lucky – you've had a severe concussion from being blown to the ground by the explosion, and we think it has affected your sight. However, our consulting ophthalmic surgeon believes the damage is temporary and he expects your eyesight will not be permanently damaged. You should recover your sight in a few days. I know you are worried about your fireman as well. Unfortunately, he was not so lucky; he was hit in the legs by some shrapnel from the same explosion and may lose his left leg."

135

George groaned. "Oh God! Poor Lance, he is an excellent fireman and would make a fine driver."

"I understand your feelings, but at least he will live. However, I'm afraid he won't be crewing an engine again."

"But he lives for firing engines!"

"Yes, I'm sorry about that; perhaps the Great Western will be able to find him another form of work which can employ his abilities. But look, there's no use worrying about it now; both you and he must concentrate on getting as fit as possible. I don't want to sound harsh, but we need the beds."

"What the hell happened, Mr D.?" A pale Lance was lying in his hospital bed with his legs immobilized. George was sitting by his bedside.

"They don't quite know, Lance. Some kind of tiny aircraft with a bomb is what I heard. But you have to try and get yourself mended; don't worry about what happened."

"They say I might lose me leg. How can I fire with only one leg?"

George was silent for a moment; he knew such a thing would be impossible.

"The doctors are not always right, Lance. You might not."

"No, you're right. I'll show the buggers, I'll be walkin' again before you can say 'Bob's your uncle.'"

"That's the spirit! Keep your pecker up."

"Me pecker's the last thing on me mind at the moment, although..." Lance paused thoughtfully, "There's one of the nurses, Annette, who's – oh, 'ere she comes!"

An attractive nurse came in and pulled out a thermometer from her pocket.

"I just need to check your temperature and pulse rate, Lance, won't be a moment."

She bent down to position the thermometer in the patient's mouth and George noticed how Lance tried to raise his head so that he could squint down inside the front of her uniform as she bent to put her finger on his pulse.

George laughed in spite of himself, "Lance, you're already

on the way to recovery."

The nurse looked at him in surprise. "Why do you say that?"

"Oh, er – nothing, it's just that my mate here is more cheerful than I would have expected."

The nurse smiled at Lance and nodded, "Yes, he's usually cheerful which all helps."

She wrote the details on the list at the end of the bed and went over to another patient.

But the doctor to whom George spoke later commented, "I'm sure he'll walk again, but he'll need an artificial leg to do it with; and as for firing railway engines, I'm afraid he can forget that!"

It was five weeks before George was declared fit enough to report to the foreman at Chester shed and to have a new fireman assigned to him.

"I'm very glad to see you back, George," said Sid Thomson, "But it's a crying shame about young Lance. Like you, I had a lot of time for him, even though he was a cheeky sod. I've given you Gwynne Evans to fire for you; he's only a Passed Cleaner, and you'll have to get him up to scratch."

Passed Cleaner Evans was keen enough to learn and a pleasant lad, but he was uneasy in his firing whenever there was some duff coal or a shortage of steam. After a couple of days with him, George had to request that the shed foreman did not give them any passenger or fitted freight duties until the fireman had acquired more skill and confidence. George could see many months of training the new lad before he could relax again in his cab, and even then he doubted that Gwynne would ever make a competent fireman.

In short, George badly missed the banter, wit and sheer ability of Fireman Hargreaves.

18 - Cleaner Evans finds his niche (October 1944)

George Denton sighed quietly as his fireman, Passed Cleaner Gwynne Evans, climbed down from the cab of their old 43xx class Mogul locomotive to ask the bobby in the signal box how much longer he was going to keep their coal train in the refuge.

They had been there for half an hour already, and were nearing the end of their shift; relief at Shrewsbury was still half an hour away from the Baschurch siding, even if they got a clear road immediately. Yet after several years of wartime hold-ups, waiting in a siding was nothing new for Driver Denton; he was more concerned about his fireman.

Gwynne Evans, a young man of medium height and generally tidy appearance, had not yet passed as a Fireman, and George had serious doubts that he ever would. Gwynne was a worrier: he worried about whether he was putting the coal in the right place in the firebox; whether the glass in the water sight gauges would break; whether the water level in the tender would last to the next water tank or troughs; whether he had picked up the right tools when going on shift. There was no doubting his efforts, but they were often poorly directed.

Asked to keep a good fire, as often as not he would pile on so much coal that he would blacken it. Not for the first time, George bitterly regretted the incident a few months back when a flying bomb had dropped on Acton Yard and sent his previous fireman, Lance Hargreaves, into hospital with what appeared to be a crippling injury. Lance had been a first-rate fireman and would have made an excellent driver in time.

George decided to have a word with the shed foreman, Sid Thomson, as to whether Gwynne could be found different work. However, the shed, like all sheds, was badly short of enginemen and needed every one they could lay their hands on, competent or not. George had little hope of getting a replacement fireman.

"We should be cleared soon," said Gwynne as he climbed back into the cab, "The bobby said that the old 28xx in front which has been holding us up has had to be stopped at Whittington with a hot box on the tender; we're being sent ahead of it."

"Thank goodness for that. OK then Gwynne, keep your eyes peeled for that signal."

"Righto," Gwynne immediately began to shovel more coal vigorously into the firebox.

George laid a restraining hand on Gwynne's arm, "Where are we going now?"

Gwynne stopped and looked up, puzzled. "Salop, I thought."

"Right, and what happens there?"

"Err... we drop the wagons off in Coleham Yard and take the old girl through the station to the GW shed?"

"Right again, and then what?"

"We book off and hope to get a lift home on the cushions?"

"But what about the engine?"

"She'll have her fire dropped and then she'll be serviced for the next duty."

George sighed, "Gwynne, I'm sorely tempted to leave you to build up that huge fire and then, when we get to the shed, tie you to the regulator."

Gwynne looked offended, asking indignantly, "What the hell for?"

"One of the fire-droppers in Salop shed is a very big bloke; when he climbs into the cab to drop the fire and sees a firebox full of fire, he's going to untie you and bung you into the firebox as well!"

Just then the signal clanged down and they were cleared to proceed onto the main line.

"Now, for the sake of your health, keep the fire low enough to get to Salop with enough steam to get to the shed and make the fire-dropper's job an easy one. It'll save your life and I won't have to witness a murder."

"Yeah," replied Gwynne thoughtfully, "Yeah, right. I'll be careful."

But Gwynne's understanding of 'careful' was such that they only just reached Coleham Yard without enough steam to go any further, as the fire was almost out. They called the yardmaster for a tow through the station to the GW shed and the driver of the shunter detailed for the job came over and climbed into the cab.

"What's up then?"

"We had some duff coal," said George. The shunter driver glanced at the three lumps of coal left in the tender and looked at George again; he nodded and climbed down.

They heard him explaining to his own fireman. "They say they've had some duff coal, but I think they've got a duff fireman!"

George and Gwynne were towed to the shed where they suffered the derision of the watching Salop enginemen from the GWR shed and even chuckles from the adjacent LMS shed.

Next day, as George came on duty, he was called over to the foreman.

"What's up, Sid?"

"I heard you had a spot of bother in Salop yesterday, George," said Sid, "What happened? They said it was duff coal, but was it Gwynne Evans again?"

Sid had received complaints about Gwynne from other drivers and knew what he was like.

"Look Sid, I don't want to ruin the lad's chances, but he's not cut out to be a fireman, let alone a driver."

"I'm afraid you're right, George, but I may have a solution; he needs more experience and we have a Passed Fireman just transferred from Milford Haven. He needs to learn the roads around here, so I'm giving him to you and Evans for a couple of weeks. His foreman tells me he's a good fireman, so your lad might learn something."

"Worth a try, I suppose," said George doubtfully.

140

Their duty that day was short freight to Oswestry, light engine back to Wrexham, and a Birkenhead stopper as far as Chester again. For this duty they were given one of the big Prairie 2-6-2s.

Morris Hughes joined them in the cab, nodding to both of them but not saying much. He was a heavily-built man with somewhat coarse features. He watched Gwynne struggling with the water hose to fill the tanks and looked at George in surprise.

"Why's he having trouble filling the tanks?" His Welsh accent was strong.

"He's still a bit new to the game; he's only just become a Passed Cleaner," replied George.

Morris said nothing and moved back as Gwynne climbed back into the cab.

They moved out into the yard to pick up the wagons.

George said to Morris, "You'd better make yourself familiar with the signals here. They're LNWR pattern until we get on to GW metals in Saltney, then it's Great Western all the way to Oswestry."

"Right," nodded Morris and he moved to sit on the bench on the left of the cab out of Gwynne's way, while Gwynne set to firing the engine. Morris noticed that the water gauge glass showed that the water in the boiler was low and waited for the young cleaner to see the problem and deal with it, but Gwynne was busy with his shovel and didn't notice.

"Oi!" snapped Morris, pointing at the gauge glass, "D'you want to drop a plug?"

"Oh... er yeah, I'll fix it in a minute," stuttered Gwynne.

"Not in a minute – NOW!" growled Morris angrily.

Gwynne dropped the shovel, reached for the injector, and began to top up the boiler. Morris watched, shaking his head.

"Take it easy, Morris, give the lad a chance," said George.

Morris grunted and watched out of the cab window for the next set of signals; he noticed drops of water falling past.

"Raining? In this weather?" He looked in the cab.

"Priming!" he called to Gwynne angrily, "You've put too much water into the boiler!"

The water from the overfilled boiler was getting into the cylinders then coming out of the chimney without doing any work. Morris looked at George but muttered quietly in Welsh.

The weather changed and it was raining hard when they dropped their light load off in Oswestry and made their way bunker-first back to Wrexham to pick up the Birkenhead stopper. George climbed down to the platform to chat to the guard about the load.

In the meantime, Gwynne picked up the oil can and was about to climb down onto the platform with it when Morris said in surprise, "What the hell are you going to do with that?"

"I thought the motion might need oiling."

"That's the driver's job, you clot! Has he told you to do that?"

"Errm... no," said Gwynne in embarrassment.

"Well, put the bloody oil can back! And check the fire and the water level!"

Gwynne climbed back up the steps, tipping the can and spilling a little oil in his haste to get back.

George finished his conversation with the guard and began to mount the footsteps to the cab. On the last step, he slipped and fell back onto the platform. When he tried to get up, he swore in a manner that Gwynne had never heard before.

"I can't stand!" he gasped, "I think my bloody ankle's broken!"

The guard helped him to a platform seat, while Morris and Gwynne looked on anxiously. Morris looked at the footplate step and saw a patch of oil on it.

"Diew, you clumsy bugger!" he exclaimed to Gwynne, "You spilt oil on the step; no wonder your driver fell!"

"This is serious," exclaimed the guard, "We'll have to

send to Croes Newydd for another driver; George here can't drive with this leg. We'll have to reckon with twenty minutes' delay – and that's only if there's a spare driver."

Morris climbed down to speak to George and the guard.

"I'm a Passed Fireman, lookyou, so I could drive and Passed Cleaner Evans here can fire and he knows the road; so we can get Driver Denton back on the cushions to Chester to get seen to there."

The guard pondered this; as guards were in charge of trains this was his responsibility. "What do you think, George?"

George nodded, wincing as he tried to stand but failed.

The guard finally nodded also, "Righto, then, let's get started."

"Wait," said George, "I should at least be in the cab where I can sit and keep an eye on things."

"We'll be fine, Mr Denton, you need to rest, and getting you up the steps would be very painful and might cause you more injury," answered Morris, "No, we'll put you into a First Class compartment where you'll be more comfortable, and we'll get you out in Chester."

Reluctantly, George agreed to this, and Morris and the guard helped him into the first coach.

"Right, my lad," said Morris, back in the cab and holding Gwynne firmly by his lapels. His face was no more than three inches from the fireman's. "You're going to fire properly. You'll do exactly as I tell you; keep the fire and boiler in good nick, an' God help you if you don't!"

Gwynne turned pale, but checked the fire and water levels.

"The water level's down a bit," he said.

Morris grabbed Gwynne's head and twisted it to face the water tower on the platform.

"You're the bloody fireman!" he snarled, "Get on the tanks and top up the water! You shouldn't need to be told."

Gwynne scrambled along the footplate, climbed onto the tank and undid the lid, before climbing back down to the platform and seizing the big rubber hose.

Morris, watching him, couldn't believe his eyes.

"What in hell are you doing?" he shouted, "That hose has a chain on it for you to pull it over; you don't have to climb down to the platform twice!"

Finally the tanks were topped up and the guard blew his whistle. Morris gently lifted the regulator and the train moved off. He was still shaking his head at Gwynne's antics.

Even to Gwynne's untutored eyes, it was clear that the train was in competent hands. Morris handled the controls with a confidence that Gwynne envied.

"When's that steep bank we have to descend?"

Gwynne thought for a moment. "It starts in a few minutes, when we begin to pass the coal mines on the right."

Morris merely nodded.

"Then there's a flat section past Rossett before we come to the climb up to Saltney Junction where we join the LMS main line. After that it's all pretty flat into Chester."

They stopped briefly at Gresford and continued down the bank and onto the plain past Rossett. As they began to ascend the Saltney bank, Morris frowned; the engine wasn't pulling as it should.

He gave a quick glance into the firebox, looked at Gwynne and growled, "D'you know what the fire should look like? You've got a great hole on the right hand side; for God's sake get it filled, or we'll never get up this bank!"

Gwynne immediately tried to shovel coal to fill the gap, but his first shovelful contained a large lump which jammed in the firehole.

"Good God almighty, man!" shouted Morris, "Get the coal pick and break it up quickly before the damn train stops on the bank!"

It took four blows before Gwynne could break up the lump; by this time the train was almost stopped and they barely reached Saltney Halt. The short stop gave Gwynne time to put in a few more shovelfuls to even out the fire so that they could get to Chester, where they arrived ten minutes late. Morris was fuming when they booked off duty, after looking after George and taking him to the First Aid centre.

Morris stared at Gwynne and shook his fist.

"Just you wait until tomorrow," he muttered, "Passed Cleaner or not, I'll bloody well sort you out properly!'

Gwynne was shaking and very unhappy at the prospect. Instead of booking off duty, he went over to the foreman's office and asked to speak to him.

"Sir, I would like you to release me from railway service. I want to join the Army and can't do so without your written permission."

Sid Thomson studied him for a while and then said, "Yes, I'll sign your release form. You've never been happy here and haven't really got what it takes to be an engineman. I trust you'll have better luck in the Army. We all wish you well."

"Thank you, sir."

The following morning there was a knock on Sid Thomson's door; it was Morris Hughes.

"Look, Sid, that young cleaner Evans – he's as thick as two planks and I don't want him in the cab with me."

"Passed Fireman Hughes, you have only been here a very short while, and I have a staff of over 150 men working for me. To you, I am Mr Thomson, sir!"

"It's sorry I am, sir, I didn't mean to be disrespectful."

"Right, then I will overlook your impudence this time. Also note that *I* decide who works with you. However, you don't need to worry about young Evans – he resigned last night. He is going to join the Army. And although you didn't ask, Driver Denton is well and should be driving again soon - his leg was only badly strained."

Outside the office, Morris Hughes grunted quietly to himself, "God help the Army; the kid's totally useless!"

He was disappointed to find himself only on shunting duties with a range of drivers for the next fortnight. But when George Denton returned to driving duties, Morris Hughes was now his regular fireman.

George soon discovered that with Fireman Hughes, he had far less to worry about than he had experienced with Cleaner Evans. Morris Hughes was a very competent fireman and made life far easier, but George found it impossible to like the man; his new fireman appeared to be simply morose by nature.

Curiously, about five months later, there was a visitor to the shed. It was an Army Corporal, who asked to see Driver Denton if possible. Coincidentally, George and Morris happened to be passing Sid Thomson's office at the time and were called in.

The corporal was ex-Passed Cleaner Evans. He stood taller and was visibly broader across the shoulders. His bearing and confidence had clearly improved immensely since he had left the railway.

"Good heavens, Gwynne! You've only been in the Army a few months and a corporal already?"

"That's right, Mr Denton. The Army found out that I could shoot; I did a sniper's course. I've been in France already and am on my first home leave. I go back in two days and help to force the Jerries to surrender. I just wanted to stop by to thank you for all the help you tried to give me; I know I wasn't much good as a fireman."

"I'm just glad you found your place, Gwynne; you were always a tryer and it's nice to see you have finally succeeded," said George, expressing genuine pleasure.

"So, you found something at which you weren't bloody useless at, after all?" Morris was barely able to hide the sarcasm in his voice.

"Yes indeed, Fireman Hughes," replied Gwynne, "I had a sergeant who had faith in me; he encouraged me to try different things and had a very positive attitude. *You* could learn a lot from him."

Morris lurched forward to grab Gwynne's arm. "You cheeky young bastard!" he snarled.

But the arm wasn't there. Instead his own arm was

146

grabbed and twisted easily round and up his back.

"The Army also taught me something about unarmed combat," commented Gwynne and he pushed Morris suddenly so that the fireman stumbled and fell down. He got up, dusted himself, and walked off out of the office without a backward glance.

Gwynne smiled at his old boss. "Very sorry about that, Mr Denton and Mr Thomson, but I never did like bullies."

19 - The return of the prodigal (September 1945)

"You'd never think we won the sodding War!" Charlie Dalrymple, now a Driver, was talking to Driver George Denton as they were both going on shift; "Food is as scarce as ever. They said they'd be increasing rations as soon as the merchant ships could get through without being attacked."

"Give 'em a chance, Charlie," replied George, "The War's only been over a month or two, and my missus and I want to see our son back from the Far East before we start complaining about the food."

"Yeah, I s'pose you're right," admitted Charlie reluctantly. "It's just that..."

"George, a word please," Sid Thomson the shed foreman called over from his office as the two men walked past.

"See you later, Charlie." George turned and walked over to the foreman's office.

"What can I do for you, Sid?"

Sid beckoned George inside and as both men were sitting down, Sid said, "Your Welsh Passed Fireman Morris Hughes is being transferred to Neyland next week. He's now a Driver; he was examined last week and wants to get back to Wales."

"He's passed his driving exam? He didn't tell me he was going for it."

"What d'you reckon to him?"

"He'll make a competent driver, but I pity any fireman who works with him; he's a miserable so-an-so and I can't say I'll be sorry to lose him. Still, I can understand him wanting to get back home."

"Well fortunately, I've got a replacement for you; I've had a request for a fireman to transfer from Didcot. He's due here tomorrow, he can replace Passed Fireman – I beg his pardon - *Driver* Hughes. You've had a fair few regular firemen since you came to Chester in er - when was it? '37?"

"Yes, March '37; yes, I must have had a dozen or more."

"Many good ones?"

"Oh yes, several: Marty Smith was a bloke I got to like after he saved that ammunition train all on his own; then I had a young Australian lad, who was over here when the War broke out and couldn't get back; but by far the best was young Lance Hargreaves before that Doodlebug came down at Acton. I was really sorry to lose him; he'd have made a cracking driver one day if he'd been able to stay with us. What's this new bloke like?"

"I haven't had much detail as yet George, but you can ask him yourself tomorrow when I get the links rearranged."

"Here you are George, and you're welcome to the bloody thing!"

The voice came from Ted Simmons leaning out of the cab as he slowly backed a large and brand new passenger engine from the turntable, to hand it over after servicing.

Ted stopped the engine, screwed on the brake and climbed down from the cab then turned to George, "I remember the disappointment we had with the new Manors when they came out in '38. Well those fatheads in Swindon have done it again; these big Counties are the same. They look good and have a greater tractive effort even than a Castle, but they won't keep time. If I can't have a Castle on the Margate with ten on, give me an old Star or a Saint any day. I was talking to some of the Salop boys, and they said the same thing; they don't like 'em at all."

"Yes, the Counties are temperamental," answered George, "And I'm getting a new fireman today, so he'll just have to learn to handle them."

"Oh? Who've you got?"

"Don't know yet, Sid's doing the rota now."

"Good luck then." Ted turned and walked away to the

shed. George climbed up into the cab and began to check the gauges. As he was doing this, he heard someone climbing the footsteps to the cab.

"What 'ave we got here then, Mr D.?" The familiar voice made George jump round and stare at the newcomer.

"Lance Hargreaves, you young devil! Where on Earth did you spring from? I thought you were finished with the railways after that flying bomb!"

"I thought so too, but after I 'ad six months in 'ospital, they said I could reck-, reack- erm... get better if I was careful."

"'Recuperate' is the word you want." George was grinning broadly and shaking Lance by the hand. "Six months in hospital? I bet none of the nurses were virgins when you left!"

"Yeah, well there was Annette; she 'ad nice knockers, an' then there was Gladys with legs a mile long, and after that there was Beryl who was always keen to - ah, you don't want to know about them. The Great Western took me back at Didcot for a while to get back into practice as it were. But what's this engine we're in? I've not seen one of these 'ere Counties before; fancy-looking engine."

"Yes they look nice, but the blokes generally don't think much of them. They're rough and they run out of steam easily and the cylinders tend to beat the boiler, but actually, I like them. They need very careful handling, but once you've got the hang of them, they're damn good for heavy passenger trains on the hilly runs. Anyway, what're you doing here?"

"Mr Thomson said you needed a fireman to help you out in your old age, so I volunteered."

George laughed. "Sid never said that! You haven't changed, you cheeky young beggar! But I'm very glad to see you because we're taking the heavy 11.35 Paddington and you'll need to bend your back."

"Ready an' willin'!"

"Right then, get your mind off nurses' knockers and back on your shovel; and you won't be so lippy by the time we reach Stafford Road shed!"

An hour later, with the 11.35 to Paddington, George opened up the regulator as they began to descend a short bank after leaving LMS metals at Saltney Junction.

"We'll need to pick up plenty of speed across the plain to get up Gresford Bank; you can top up when we stop at Wrexham and build the fire up again."

"Gotcha!" acknowledged Lance with enthusiasm as he bent to load up the shovel from the tender. The express gradually built up speed as they crossed the Cheshire plain, with Lance shovelling hard and placing the coal carefully around the firebox and building up the classic haycock-style fire which the Great Western engines seemed to thrive on.

They gradually lost momentum on climbing Gresford Bank and Lance began to place his coal to fill up the holes in the fire that the engine's hard steaming was rapidly creating. He was thankful when he sighted the signals for the stop at Wrexham.

"Hey up, Mr D.," he said, staring out of the window to the oncoming platform, "There's a bunch of coppers waiting – somethin' must be up."

As they stopped, a grim-faced police constable moved towards them and climbed up into the cab.

"I hope you're not going to keep us," grumbled George as he reached for his notebook in the roof shelf and filled in his timekeeping details, "We're on time now, and we..."

"I want to know why you killed a harmless old man, you bastard!"

The policeman grabbed hold of Lance's arm and turned to George, snarling, "Or was it you? Which one of you sods was it?"

This was too much for Lance who, although he was shorter than the policeman, grabbed his wrist, forced the man's arm up behind his back and turned him round.

"What the 'ell d'yer think yer doin'?" Lance growled, "Just tell me before I throw yer off the bloody cab!"

Unnoticed by all three men, another figure appeared at the top of the cab steps.

151

"Alright, settle down everyone," he said in a quiet voice that nevertheless stopped everyone in their tracks.

He addressed George, "I'm sorry for this unseemly behaviour on the part of my constable, Driver, but a man has been killed and we need to question all those involved."

He then spoke to the constable. 'Thank you, P.C. Harris, I think it would be best if you left me to ask the questions."

"But sir, these buggers..."

"That'll be all, constable. Now go and interview some passengers, they might have seen what happened."

"Well I should arrest this one for assaulting a police officer!"

"It was self-defence; you seized him first. Now off you go."

Grumbling, the constable climbed down and stalked off down the platform to the first coach, where he opened the door and entered.

The man nodded to Lance and George and showed them his warrant card.

"Detective Inspector Henshawe. As I said, I'm really sorry about that, but my constable has a point; a pedestrian was killed by your train at Balderton a short while ago and we have to find out how this happened."

"Well, I'm sorry, Inspector, we can't help you. We didn't see anyone at Balderton; we don't stop there."

"No, I understand that. The pedestrian was on the level crossing when your train hit him. You didn't see him at all?"

"No, but the gates must have been closed to road traffic because we were signalled clear through the station."

"Yes, they were; we think he must have climbed over the gates and tried to cross."

"Well Lance was firing, so he wouldn't have seen anyone, and I was driving but I can only see the right hand side, of course. If the man was on the left hand side, neither of us would have seen him. And then, even if we had, it wouldn't have made any difference."

"Oh? And why not?"

"Well," said George, "With a 350 ton train racing at 65 miles an hour, we couldn't possibly stop inside half a mile, even with the emergency brake on."

"Mmm..." mused the Detective Inspector, "No, I see that. But we'll have to examine the front of the locomotive. We'll be as quick as we can."

A cursory check of the buffer beam showed traces of blood on the left, but nothing else, and George was given permission to continue.

Lance concentrated on firing and was uncommonly subdued as they drove on through Ruabon and Gobowen to Shrewsbury, trying to make up lost time.

"There's nowt we could've done, Mr D.," he said, "Even if we'd seen 'im."

"No," answered George, "But remember, he chose to ignore common sense. You can't legislate against stupidity. The only victims here are his family, his friends and us."

"Us?"

"Of course. We have to live with the knowledge that we killed a man; that's not easy. Thankfully, it doesn't happen very often that people are killed on railway tracks, but when they are, the public is full of sympathy for those injured. They don't pay much attention to the unfortunate – and normally blameless - engine crews. Some drivers can no longer face driving after an incident like that and they lose their careers through no fault of their own. But for the motormen on the electrics, it's far worse; they see it coming – it's right under their noses - and they can do nothing about it."

"'As this ever 'appened to you before?"

"Yes once, in 1931. I was firing a fitted freight near Taunton when a tramp ran across the rails in front of me; he was being chased by a policeman and burst out of a copse and was on the track before we could react."

"'Ow did you feel after that?"

"Pretty grim, but I'd seen far worse as a soldier in the Great War, so it didn't affect me as much as it might have."

When George and Lance booked off duty at Stafford Road shed, they reported to the foreman, who had been informed of the incident. He expressed his sympathy for them, as did many of their colleagues; even those they didn't know. There was a bond between enginemen because they all faced the same risks whenever they climbed into the cab.

The following day they were scheduled for shunting. Although Lance had coped with the heavier work firing on the County, he was glad of an easier day shift; shunting normally meant plenty of pauses between marshalling vans and trucks, and firing the smaller Pannier locomotives under these circumstances was no trouble. He was surprised therefore to see his driver with a gloomy face coming on duty.

"You still thinkin' about that bloke yesterday?"

"That and other things."

"What other things?"

"Have you seen what we're driving today?"

"Yeah; a little Pannier – Number 1987. Mr Thomson ses it may be old, but it's bin reconditioned and in good nick."

"Oh yes, it's in good nick alright; I was on it a fortnight ago."

"So what's the problem?"

"Can't you guess?"

Lance was puzzled. "No."

"Well," said George looking at the dark sky, "You'll find out in about half an hour."

"Oh!" said Lance, "it's one o' them old tankies with only 'alf a cab roof."

"Ah!" replied George, "The penny's dropped."

"But we've bin in plenty of Saints and Stars, an' their cabs aren't much bigger."

"True," and George eyed Lance with a questioning look, "And what were we doing in them?"

Lance shrugged, "Running passenger trains?"

"True again, but when you're speeding along, you get some protection from the rain. In a shunting stint, we're standing about getting wet."

They climbed into the cab and Lance began checking the gauges. Their first job was to break up a newly arrived freight from Hereford. George's prediction about the weather bore fruit an hour later. They were standing waiting for a Birkenhead stopper with a couple of parcels vans to remove when the downpour came.

"Gawd, it's pissin' down!" grumbled Lance, trying in vain to keep himself dry and warm by pressing up against the boiler backhead. But the rain had no mercy and the two enginemen spent a miserable shift soaked to the skin as they shunted vans and wagons around the Chester yard. As they trudged back to the shed to clock off after eight hours of being wet through, George grinned at Lance.

"Still happy to be back firing?" he asked, but only got a bad-tempered grunt in reply.

The following day, as if to apologize for its previous bad behaviour, the weather was bright and sunny. George and Lance were once more on an express to Paddington and again had another new County class locomotive to work with.

"Remember what I told you about firing these engines, Lance?" asked George.

"Yep!" answered Lance, who appeared to have recovered his good mood once more, "The classic 'aycock fire an' we'll be right as ninepence!"

Lance began to make up the fire as required as they travelled over the Dee Bridge and through the Curzon Park cutting on the LMS North Wales down relief line, before curving left at Saltney junction to join the Great Western main line south.

Speeding again through Balderton station, both men kept a nervous eye on the track ahead, remembering the tragedy of a couple of days earlier, but there was no sign of anything untoward. Using the stops at Wrexham and Ruabon to replenish the fire as the heavy train took its toll, Lance paused to look out over the beautiful Dee valley. They crossed the long viaduct at Chirk and Lance began to pile on the coal for the longer stretch between Gobowen and Shrewsbury as George began to build up speed. Racing through Whittington, the engine was burning up coal almost as fast as Lance could shovel it into the firebox.

Occasionally Lance paused in his firing to look up at his driver with a wide grin over his face. "Jeez, d'yer know, Mr D., in spite of that nasty accident the other day, I've missed this! I've bin itchin' to get back to this lark!"

"You're really enjoying yourself, aren't you!"

"Bloody marvellous!" said Lance and bent his back again, throwing more coal into the firebox as the train thundered through Leaton. He paused and glanced out of the cab as the fields and farmhouses flashed past.

"Me cousin drives a twenty-ton army tank at fifteen miles an hour," he chuckled, "An' 'e ses it's great. I told 'im, 'e should try driving a 'undred-ton engine with 350 tons on its tail beltin' along at seventy miles an hour!"

20 – George assists once more (June 1960)

Driver Lance Hargreaves walked in and dropped his lunch box on the bench at Wolverhampton Stafford Road Shed.

In spite of his relatively young age, Lance was one of the most respected drivers at the shed; he was in the top link and normally used to the very demanding duties of the Bristol trains, heavy Paddington expresses and driving the Kings; among the most powerful express locomotives in the country and pride of the ex-GWR fleet. These engines had recently been re-draughted at Swindon works and the alterations were turning the thirty-year-old engines into machines that could match anything newer that the other three regions of British Railways had to offer.

Earlier that day, the foreman had said to him, "Lance, Frank Woodford is learning the road to Chester and I want you to take him with you on the Birkenhead this morning. I've given you 1016 for it."

1016 was a County class locomotive and a regular on this run. Lance nodded his agreement, but he knew Frank and so far, he hadn't been very impressed.

When he first heard about them taking Frank, Harry Paisley, Lance's fireman, also expressed a certain disappointment: "Frank Woodford? Do we have to? Frank's an arsehole!"

Lance looked at his fireman, "Of course he's an arsehole; almost everyone's an arsehole for somebody. I'm sure Frank thinks you're an arsehole too! And I'll bet if you mention my name to the shedmaster at Hereford, he'd tell you I'm a prize arsehole."

"Why, Mr H.? What did you do to upset him?"

Lance grinned at Harry, "That's for me to know and for you to find out!"

Frank Paisley climbed into the cab, and the two firemen, in spite of their mutual animosity, were civil to

157

each other; they both knew Lance and were well aware of his possible reaction if there were any ructions in his cab. Lance was widely respected as an excellent driver, but it was equally well known that he didn't suffer fools gladly and was liable to take drastic action if need be.

Frank was clearly impressed by the way Lance drove, and asked him if he liked the Counties.

"Yeah," replied Lance, "If I've got a heavy train as far as Chester I wouldn't want anything else."

"But what about a Castle?" Frank wanted to know, "They're better than Counties, which I know many of the Salop men don't like at all."

"For sustained long heavy pulling, I'd agree; give me a Castle or a King anytime; but if you've got a hilly road and a heavy train on this run or the Cornish run between Plymouth and Penzance, you can't beat a County. They do tend to run out of steam quickly, but you can recover well enough down the hills and at the stops. They pull uphill very well, especially now they've been modified. Mind you," he added, "Once with George Denton driving, we had an old Saint on this run just before they were all scrapped and it did us proud."

"Lance, for God's sake, why aren't you in the platform? You're ten minutes late!" A locomotive inspector stormed up to the engine where Lance, his fireman and an observer were chatting in the cab.

"What? Oh crikey, my watch must have stopped!" Lance took his watch out of his fob pocket, stared at it and then lifted the regulator, before popping the watch back into his pocket.

The engine moved off shed slowly towards the station where the 11.35 had brought eleven bogies from Chester. The County class engine had already uncoupled and was waiting to back into the shed for servicing. Lance's King backed on to the waiting four coaches and added them to the Paddington train which now left ten minutes late.

Simon Poulton was a London driver in the cab, learning the road in preparation for running the diesels which were expected to take over from the steam locomotives within a few years. He looked at Lance curiously, but said nothing.

In Birmingham Snow Hill, Lance muttered about a leaking gland and had to go the front of the engine to check, then returning, saying it was nothing. As a consequence, they left Snow Hill twelve minutes late.

By Leamington, Lance had managed to reduce the delay by three minutes and had a gleam in his eye as they pulled out of the station.

"You're going to bend your back a bit, Harry," he remarked to his fireman, "We've got a bit of catching up to do."

"OK, Mr H., let 'er rip!" said Harry, who knew what Lance could do with a King in good nick. They raced southwards and Simon noticed with interest that the speedometer touched 100 mph a couple of times; they only slowed down through Bicester and then picked up speed again.

Some time later, the Paddington stationmaster in his top hat strolled over to a platform inspector he saw for a chat.

"Bit different from Newton Abbot, wouldn't you say?" he asked him.

"Er - Yessir," answered the inspector.

"You look like you have a problem?"

"Well, I've just heard that the Birkenhead is running twelve minutes late from Snow Hill."

"Oh? Do you know who's crewing?"

The inspector looked in his notebook. "Er - yes; Driver Hargreaves and Fireman Paisley. Be a blot on their copybooks."

"I doubt it," said the stationmaster.

"But picking up twelve minutes, sir, with a heavy express on what is only a two-hour journey; they'll never make that. I know the road is hilly and there are several speed restrictions."

The stationmaster took off his hat and said, "Are you a

betting man?"

"I've had the occasional flutter."

The stationmaster took five shillings out of his pocket and dropped them into his hat. "Five bob says they'll be here on time."

The inspector grinned, "You're on, sir." He dropped another five shillings into the hat and looked at his watch, "And I'll be collecting my winnings in three minutes!"

The stationmaster pointed with his hat down the track.

The inspector looked as well. Disbelief clouded his face. A King was slowly approaching the platform with its fifteen carriages snaking behind it across the points and crossings to enter the platform. It slowed down as it approached the two men then glided to a gentle stop a yard or two from the hydraulic buffers.

"Problem, Lance," said Simon, looking out of the cab as they pulled in.

"What?"

Simon had seen the Paddington stationmaster in his top hat waiting on their platform near the buffers. As they stopped, the stationmaster swung himself into the cab with a smile on his face.

"Hold out your hand, Lance!" he said and dropped two florins and a shilling into Lance's hand.

"What's that for, sir?"

"I was talking to a new loco inspector who has transferred here from the Newton Abbot Division. He told me you had made a timing error and were running twelve minutes late out of Snow Hill with a heavy train. I bet him five shillings you'd be here right time. He didn't believe me; he does now - five bob is your share!"

As they backed off to Ranelagh Road for turning, Lance asked Simon if he'd learned much of the road.

"That's not all I've learned," replied Simon, "I've also learned that you're a crafty bugger!"

"What're you talking about?"

"Your watch hadn't stopped; I noticed you took care not

to let the Stafford Road loco inspector see it; but I saw it!" he said with a broad grin on his face. "And in Snow Hill, you knew there was no leaking gland – you just wanted to lose a few more minutes!"

"Why would I want to do that?" Lance's face was all innocence.

"Two reasons: you wanted to show me that a steamer could still manage as well as a big diesel; and you wanted an excuse to get your King to do a hundred miles an hour!"

"Seems I'm not the only crafty bugger in the business!"

"Mind you, I have to admit too, you're a bloody good driver."

Lance gazed unseeing into the distance, "Mmmh... yes," he nodded, "I was very lucky, I learned from the best. I reckon my regular driver in the '40s, George Denton, was the finest driver in the whole Division. Never once did I see him caught out with a problem on the engine he couldn't solve."

"Oh, George Denton! I met him once just before he retired in... err, when was it?"

"1952."

"Yeah, that's right. He brought his grandson to the shed because the lad was mad keen on railways."

"Yes," nodded Lance, "George asked me once to try and persuade the boy not to join the railways."

"Can't say I blame him," agreed Simon, "No future in railways these days, I'm thinking."

Lance had met George Denton Junior for the first time five years back, when the boy had come with his father, Ben, to visit George Senior.

The former driver had asked Lance to take his twelve-year-old grandson on a cab ride, to show him how dirty the job was. Uncle Lance had agreed and, while out on the tracks, had tried to dissuade the boy from joining the railways.

"You won't be a steam engine driver, young George," he had stated, "By the time you start work, the steamers'll be on the way out. British Railways has a new policy of diesels and electrics – not the same at all. Very clean, mind you, but without the magic of these," he patted the backhead of the old Star class express passenger engine they found themselves in.

Lance continued, "And this old beauty here's for the scrapyard in two months, and she's one of the last in her class."

"But the wonderful Kings, Uncle Lance, they're just being done up! They wouldn't scrap them."

"They've only got five or six more years, George, then they'll be gone as well. The Castles and Counties won't last much longer. The first diesels are coming in already, in five or six years' time there won't be a steamer on the Western at all..."

"But, but..." A tear could be seen welling up in the youngster's eye.

"And people are using cars more these days," Lance continued, "How did your Dad come up from Stafford?"

"Well, yeah, we came by car."

"There's another thing too," Lance continued, "Railway pay is not good these days compared to the pay in many other jobs, I'm sorry to say."

"What will you do, Uncle Lance?"

"I'll have to learn to drive the diesels; I've no choice, I've been a driver all my life. Even a diesel cab would be better than sitting in an office. But I won't say I'll enjoy it."

Later, Lance's ex-driver had said to him, "Many thanks, Lance for putting my grandson off a railway job, there's not much future in it, and Ben is really grateful to you. He wants George to try and get into university; his teachers tell him George's school results are very good."

Lance was by now a driver in the top link at Stafford Road shed in Wolverhampton. He had a small flat in the town and he had moved there because he wanted to get his hands on the big King class locomotives, which were not permitted north to Chester as they were too heavy for the Gresford Bank with its load restriction. Shrewsbury was their limit and even that was only a recent development.

He still visited Chester frequently because he liked to keep in contact with his old driver; the two had been mates for many years and were still close friends, especially since the death of George's wife. Lance would have a meal with George at a local restaurant and they would then spend an hour or so reminiscing at George's local pub.

But there was another reason for Lance's frequent visits to Chester: a young single mother in Chester had a five-year-old boy who always looked forward to visits from his 'Uncle Lance', to whom he bore a remarkably close resemblance.

On his last visit, Lance had taken the opportunity to call on the young mother again.

"Listen, Sal, I'm thinking of moving back to Chester," he said to her.

"Why? You can't drive your Kings here, you'd hate that."

"It would be a blow," admitted Lance, "But living so far away from you and the lad isn't any fun either."

"You seriously mean you'd give up those great engines for us?"

Lance shrugged, "I love the job of course, but I feel I've been missing something else more important; I'm not seeing you and the boy enough and want to be much closer to you both than I have been."

"But we've been through all that many times already. Remember, it was my fault to begin with; I'm not going to hold you to it."

"No, I know that love, but..."

"And there's something else," she began, "I've handed in my notice at work. I start a new job next month."

"What job... and where?"

"The same sort of work, but... well, we're going to have to move from Chester."

Lance was horrified, "Where to?"

"Wolverhampton... and you're going to have to find a house for us to... oof!"

Sally gasped, as Lance lifted her up and kissed her.

163

Their return trip from Paddington on the 2.10 was less eventful to begin with but as they slowed down on the approach to the Wednesbury curve, Simon called out, "You've got the home and distant clear, Lance, you can open her up."

However, Lance hesitated and continued to slow the train.

"What's up? Why aren't you accelerating?" queried Simon.

"There's something wrong," said Lance frowning, "I'm not sure what it is yet, but... Oh shit!" he cried as they rounded the curve to find two or three derailed trucks blocking their rails.

Lance slammed on the emergency brake and the train stopped about twenty yards short of the wagon.

"It looks like a bad derailment on that siding," muttered Lance, climbing down the cab steps to walk to the brake van and view the damage. They had a twenty minute wait while the damaged truck was removed from the down main line and the express could proceed.

Later, back in the cab, Simon asked, "How the holy hell did you know not to accelerate? That derailment was round the curve, out of sight, and had only just occurred! If you'd been speeding we would have had a serious accident, possibly even with some fatalities!"

Harry, staring at his driver, asked quietly, "George Denton again?"

"Yeah," nodded Lance slowly.

"George Denton?" asked Simon in surprise, "What's he got to do with this?"

"It's funny," answered Lance, "But on very rare occasions I seem to hear George's voice in my head warning me about some danger. I heard it again just now. George taught me all I know about driving. He retired eight years back and he was fine until he lost Alice, his wife, through cancer. I think that hit him very hard. I still visit him every few weeks."

Simon took out his watch, "Well, we stopped twenty minutes ago in the afternoon on... er... let me see... the fifteenth of May. Next time you see George, ask him what he was doing today at four-oh-seven!"

It was clear that Simon had no time for the unexplainable.

Back in Stafford Road shed, Lance checked their roster for the following day.

"12.12 to Chester, Harry," he chuckled, "Gets in at 2.21 and back on the 9.45. That gives me time to have a cup of tea with George Denton and ask him what he was doing today!"

But before clocking off, Lance was called into the night shift foreman's office.

"Glad I caught you, Lance," the foreman said, "There's a phone call for you. Take it here and I'll leave you to it."

The foreman left the office and Lance picked up the phone, "Lance Hargreaves."

"Ben Denton here, Lance. I've got very bad news; it's Dad."

"What's wrong, Ben? I was going to see your Dad tomorrow."

Ben sighed, "He had a stroke yesterday and was taken in to the Royal Infirmary."

"Oh hell, Ben, I am so sorry. Of course I'll go and see him."

There was a pause before Ben spoke.

"You can't, Lance. He had a turn for the worse this afternoon and passed away, shortly after four o'clock."

The Engines

Steam locomotives were classified according to their wheel arrangements: the basis was the number of wheels used for driving, with other numbers used for small guiding wheels at the front and rear trailing wheels.

For instance, a 4-6-2 had a set of four small wheels in front of the drivers, to guide the engine round curves, six main driving wheels, and another set of two wheels at the rear to help take the weight. An 0-6-0 had only six driving wheels and no others.

Engines were also classed according to their purpose, e.g. express passenger, heavy freight, mixed traffic (i.e. passenger or freight), or shunting.

Locomotives of the same design were also grouped under the name of the design.

GWR

King class: The premier express passenger engine of the company. It handled all the heaviest express passenger trains from Paddington to either Plymouth or Wolverhampton. The 4-6-0s were restricted to these routes because of their great weight. Visually very similar to Castles.

Castle class: The largest class of express passenger locomotives. They were strong and fast 4-6-0s.

Star class: 4-6-0s and precursors to the Castle class. Strong and powerful and generally popular with their crews, but by the 1940s they were wearing out. Known as 'Forties' due to their numbers beginning 40xx.

Saint class: Similar to the Star class but with only two, not four, cylinders. Not quite so strong. These 4-6-0s were known as '29s'.

Hall class: These were extremely useful 4-6-0 general purpose locomotives and were found on most main routes of the Company's system.

County class: These were heavy general purpose 4-6-0 locomotives but were only built at the end of World War II. Initially not popular with many enginemen, but when modified they became very suited to hilly main lines.

Grange class: Another 4-6-0 general purpose engine, lighter and with smaller wheels, slightly more powerful than the Halls.

Manor class: Light 4-6-0 general purpose engines. Initially, as with the Counties, not successful, but once modified they became excellent engines for more lightly-laid routes.

Bulldog class: An early class of 4-4-0 general purpose engines with outside frames which made them appear obsolete, but in fact they were useful little engines.

47xx: Heavy 2-8-0 express freight locomotive occasionally used on passenger trains.

28xx: Heavy 2-8-0 standard freight locomotive.

Aberdare: Elderly 2-6-0 freight locomotives, mostly due for scrapping but kept on during World War II.

Mogul: Mixed traffic 2-6-0 locomotives. Known as the 43xx class.

Prairie: Mixed traffic 2-6-2 tank locomotives.

Pannier: Light 0-6-0 tank engines with square tanks on either side of the boiler.

Other companies' engines

LMS

Duchess: Large 4-6-2 (Pacific) locomotives for heavy express work. Some were originally streamlined but this feature was later removed for ease of maintenance.

Royal Scot class: Express passenger 4-6-0 locomotives corresponding roughly to the Castles of the GWR. They were completely rebuilt in the 1940s and 1950s.

Patriot class: Medium-powered 4-6-0s for express passenger and parcels trains.

Black Five class: A medium-powered general purpose 4-6-0 and popular with enginemen as they were extremely versatile. They were Stanier's LMS version of the GWR 'Hall' class.

Jinty: Small 0-6-0 general purpose and shunting engine.

Glossary

For those less familiar with a few of the terms used by railwaymen of the first half of the twentieth century.

Banker: Extra engine used at the back of a train to assist it uphill.

Bay platform: Platform with a buffer stop at one end.

Blow-back: Rare burst of fire into the cab.

Bobby: Signalman.

Bogies: Railway term for coaches. Also a set of four or six wheels in a frame.

Brake van: Small van at the end of a goods train from which the guard could apply a brake to assist the driver when slowing the train. In a passenger train, the brake van would be a coach with a section for the guard.

Cleaner: Apprentice engine cleaner preparing to become first a fireman then later a driver.

Clinker: Partly-burned coal remnants which would stick to the grate and needed to be removed to allow air through the fire to aid combustion.

Corridors: Railway term for coaches used in longer-distance trains. They had corridors with toilets, as opposed to the non-corridor trains used for short distances.

Clear: A signal which indicates that the route ahead is clear for a train to proceed.

Control: The department of the railway company responsible for managing crewing of trains.

Detonators: Small explosive devices placed on the track to warn approaching trains in an emergency. On hearing detonators, a driver would stop immediately.

Distant signal: The signal giving warning of the status of the next section of track but one. Normally yellow with a black chevron stripe.

Down: The route direction away from London (see also 'Up').

Driver: The man responsible for driving the locomotive.

Empty Coaching Stock (ECS): A train of empty coaches to be taken where they were needed. These trains were not advertised in the public timetables and did not carry passengers.

Firebox: The section of the locomotive immediately in front of the cab, in which the fire would be situated.

Fireman: The man responsible for keeping the fire at a level sufficient to maintain enough steam for the driver to drive.

Fitted goods: A goods train fitted with vacuum brakes, which would allow it to travel at higher speeds than an unfitted goods.

Fouling point: The point in a siding at which a stabled train is clear of the main line.

Guard: The man in charge of a train. He travelled in the brake van at the rear of a goods train or passenger train.

Headshunt: Extra siding to allow a locomotive to wait before backing onto a train or to permit a shunting operation without interfering with station or yard approach tracks.

Home signal: The signal controlling the next section of track. Normally red with a white stripe.

Hot box: Hot axle box of a vehicle filled with grease or oil; if it got too hot it could start a fire.

Injector: Pump in a steam locomotive to force water into the boiler.

Knocker up: A cleaner who would be used to wake up enginemen when they were needed on shift.

Light engine: An engine without a train.

Loose coupled: A train of goods vehicles fitted only with metal couplings and thus limited to a speed of 40 mph.

Loop: Side track to allow a train to be marshalled for departure or after arrival without blocking the main line.

Main: Tracks for fast trains.

Metals: Rails or tracks.

Non-corridors: Coaches used in short distance trains did not normally have their compartments connected by corridors.

Passed Cleaner/Fireman: Cleaner or fireman who had

satisfied the authorities that he could be trained for promotion to the next rank. He could be used as a fireman/driver under training.

Pilot engine: Engine which would be added in front of a train engine and used to assist with a heavy train.

Plug: A fusible lead plug in the boiler which would melt if the water level sank too low, thus releasing steam pressure to prevent the boiler from exploding.

Regulator: Large lever in the cab of locomotives, enabling the driver to regulate the flow of steam to the cylinders, essentially controlling the speed of the train.

Semi-fast: Passenger train which does not stop at all stations.

Shed: Depot for steam locomotives. Locomotives were allotted to a particular shed which was responsible for their day-to-day maintenance.

Shedmaster: Foreman in charge of a shed.

Shocvan: Goods van with special springs to prevent damage during shunting.

Siding: Stretch of track used to store vehicles until they were required.

Signalling: Used to control the movement of trains. A 'home' signal controlled the entry to a section. If it showed 'clear', entry was permitted. If it showed 'danger', entry was not permitted.

A 'distant' signal warned of the position of the next home signal; a clear meant that the next home signal was also clear, whereas a danger meant that the next home signal showed danger also and that the driver should prepare to stop his train at the next signal.

Slow: Tracks for slow/stopping trains.

Sole and heel: Light maintenance and repair to a locomotive.

Special: Non-timetabled train for a special purpose.

Steam heating: Most passenger trains had their coaches heated by steam pipes throughout the train.

Steam lance: Hose which could be connected to the boiler of a locomotive to force superheated steam through the boiler tubes to clear them of any blockages.

Steam pressure: The pressure of steam in the locomotive boiler.

Stopper: Passenger train which stops at most or all stations on its route.

Tank engine: Locomotive incorporating a bunker for coal and tanks for water; used for short-distance work. As tank engines could travel either smokebox- or bunker-first they did not need to turn on a turntable.

Tender: Special vehicle attached behind a steam locomotive to carry the coal and water needed.

35-tonners: Railway term for coaches. Thirty five tons was the standard weight of most coaches.

Unfitted goods: Goods train in which the vehicles are not fitted with vacuum brakes. See also 'loose coupled'.

Up: The route direction towards London.

Water troughs: Long metal troughs filled with water between the rails to allow locomotives to pick up water at speed.

Wheel tapper: Metallurgy expert who tapped the wheels of vehicles with a special hammer to listen for metal fatigue.

Common abbreviations

CLC: Cheshire Lines Committee; a small private railway company in Lancashire and Cheshire serving Liverpool, Manchester and Chester. HQ at Liverpool Central.

ECS: Empty Coaching Stock

GWR: Great Western Railway; a private railway company serving the West of England, South Wales and north as far as Birkenhead and Warrington. HQ at Paddington.

LMS: London, Midland and Scottish Railway; serving western and central England, the north-west and Scotland. HQ at Euston.

LNER: London and North Eastern Railway; serving eastern and north-eastern England and Scotland. HQ at King's Cross.

LT: London Transport; the authority for most Public transport in London, the Underground, buses, and trams.

SR: Southern Railway; serving the south and south-west of England. HQ at Waterloo.

Acknowledgements

I am very grateful to all those who have assisted in the production of this book.

Firstly, the gentlemen of the Victorian 'O' Gauge Guild: Ian Norman must take the initial blame for it as it was he who gave me what some might consider foolish encouragement to continue with the stories.

I am also grateful for the advice and comments from Richard Davidson, John Ritter and Paul Brown, amongst others.

John Kneeshaw, editor of the *Gauge 'O' Guild Journal*, gave me very helpful publishing information and John Brown, formerly a fireman of Kidderminster, provided useful technical advice.

Thanks are also due to both Paul Brown and Richard Woodman for their invaluable cooperation in producing the cover illustration.

However, the whole book would not have been able to raise steam, as it were, had it not been for my editor, Katharine Smith. She undertook the job of editing, formatting and marketing, and looking after the business details which are vital in preparing a manuscript for publication.

Lightning Source UK Ltd.
Milton Keynes UK
UKHW040106091119
353172UK00001B/42/P